DANNY LOVES PASTA

"Danny's videos put a smile on my face every day, and this book is everything we know him for and more. Super creative, fun, and personal, but also a masterclass in everything you need to know about pasta. This book looks good on the coffee table, but you'll probably find it in the kitchen covered in flour because there's just so much to learn!"

—**POPPY O'TOOLE,** author of *Poppy Cooks: The Food You Need* and judge on Young MasterChef UK

"Gorgeously shot and so wonderfully personal, Danny injects a deeply needed sense of fun and whimsy to the oftentimes serious and methodical world of pasta. Every recipe is an encouragement to dare to try something different for no other reason than the sake of joy, which makes *Danny Loves Pasta* perfect for anyone who might want to try making pasta for the first time. Because of that same element of fun, some lifelong experts might learn a thing or two from him as well."

—**JON KUNG,** content creator and cookbook author

"Danny's ode to pasta is simply a joy. From delicate tortellini wrapped in thin multi-colored pinstripes—a genius technique that I now happily use in my own doughs—to ravioli shaped like delightful succulents, *Danny Loves Pasta* is a book that pushes the boundaries of what pasta can be in the most friendly and approachable way. Every recipe is a love letter to the art of pasta, where shapes and fillings from the traditional to whimsical have turned my kitchen into a playground of flour and creativity. The results look like edible art, but I don't stare for too long. In the end, the pasta is simply too delicious not to eat."

—**FRANKIE GAW,** author of *First-Generation* and creator of Little Fat Boy

Danny Freeman

DANNY LOVES PASTA

75+ fun and colorful pasta
shapes, patterns, sauces,
and more

Publisher Mike Sanders
Senior Editor Olivia Peluso
Editor Christopher Stolle
Art Director William Thomas
Senior Designer Jessica Lee
Photographer Rikki Snyder
Food Stylist Leslie Orlandini
Recipe Tester Trish Sebben Malone
Proofreaders Georgette Beatty & Rick Ball
Indexer Beverlee Day

First American Edition, 2023
Published in the United States by DK Publishing
DK, a Division of Penguin Random House LLC
1745 Broadway, 20th Floor, New York, NY 10019

The authorized representative in the EEA is Dorling Kindersley
Verlag GmbH. Arnulfstr. 124, 80636 Munich, Germany

Copyright © 2023 by Danny Freeman
23 24 25 26 27   10 9 8 7 6 5 4 3 2
003-335139-JUN2023

A catalog record for this book is available from the Library of Congress.
ISBN 978-0-7440-7833-6

DK books are available at special discounts when purchased in bulk
for sales promotions, premiums, fund-raising, or educational use.
For details, contact: DK Publishing Special Markets,
1745 Broadway, 20th Floor, New York, NY 10019
SpecialSales@dk.com

Printed and bound in Slovakia

For the curious
www.dk.com

This book was made with Forest
Stewardship Council ™ certified
paper - one small step in DK's
commitment to a sustainable future.
For more information go to
www.dk.com/our-green-pledge

To my parents, who have never stopped believing in me and to whom I owe everything.

Contents

CHAPTER 6: NEW SHAPES

CHAPTER 7: SAUCES

CHAPTER 8: FILLINGS

My Pasta-Making Journey

I have a photo of the very first time I ever had pasta. I was eight months old and had just started eating solid foods, and my parents gave me some spaghetti to try. And I must have really enjoyed it, because by the time my parents could grab the camera, I'd eaten all the food that had been in front of me. In the photo, though, you can see the evidence of my meal: my mother's homemade sauce smeared all over my tray, hands, bib, and cheeks. And a little up on my forehead, too. Most importantly, I have a giant smile across my face. I obviously don't remember that day, but I like to think that was the moment that my lifelong love for pasta began.

My mother is from a big Italian-American family, so perhaps it was inevitable that pasta would become my favorite food. Ours was the type of family where relatives were always stopping by, and even the smallest gatherings had enough food to feed a medium-sized army. At every holiday or celebration, we'd have all the classics—lasagna, eggplant parm, shrimp scampi, chicken cacciatore—they were always homemade, and always piping hot. And, of course, nobody left the party without a paper plate full of leftovers, wrapped in aluminum foil and shoved into their hands as they made their way to the door.

These family gatherings were an Italian-food lover's dream, but here's my embarrassing secret: Even though I had plates upon plates of food to choose from, I almost always skipped over most of it. All I really wanted to eat was a giant bowl of pasta, smothered in a homemade batch of piping hot tomato sauce. Back then, I ate this multiple times a week, and to this day, I still do; in my 36 years, I've never once gotten sick of it. Pasta was, and still is, my ultimate comfort food, the one dish I could eat over and over again.

There are many great cooks in my family who make wonderful pasta, but my grandmother's was always my favorite. Her cooking was legendary, as were most things about her. She was so unlike me in many ways: Funny and outgoing, larger than life, she could talk to anyone and they'd remember the conversation years later. As a shy, closeted gay kid growing up in Upstate New York, I was drawn to her; I felt honored to be in her presence and to be related to her. It was as if she shone brightly enough that just by standing close to her, it might look like some of the light was radiating from me, too. Once, when I was about seven, she took me to the movies and on the way in, we were stopped by the ticket agent because we each had a box of candy purchased from the convenience store down the street. "We'll just eat it outside," she said to him, but as we walked out of sight, she told me to shove my candy into my jacket. I would have been too nervous to do this on my own, as I was a rule follower by nature, but with her I felt like I could do anything.

Through acts large and small, my grandmother always made me feel loved and special. She sat through my backyard magic shows with a large smile, and she was there for every school play, every graduation, and my one ill-fated half-season on the track team. She spoke during my wedding ceremony, and she held my daughter when she was just a few weeks old. I wish everyone had a person like my grandmother in their life, someone who loves you unconditionally and always makes you

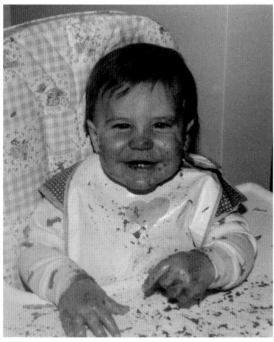

The beginning of my lifelong pasta obsession.

My grandmother making pasta for Thanksgiving, 1987.

My mother and me at my first birthday party, 1987.

My grandmother and me on Thanksgiving, 2019.

My husband Steve and me on our wedding day in Saratoga Springs, NY. ©Sarah Smith

feel special, even when you're not so sure that there's anything special about you at all.

Like many Italian grandmothers, she showed her love through food. When I was a kid, my grandparents would come over every Sunday after dinner, and she would always walk through the door with a homemade dessert and a bag of candy for me and my brothers. Whenever I would visit her as an adult, she'd always want to feed me. She would fret, "I just wish I had something I could give you to eat!" Of course, she was ignoring the leftover spaghetti, slice of pie, and random pieces of fruit that she had already given me. Every Christmas, we'd go to her house, and she'd cook up a giant feast for all our relatives. Just before it was time to eat, she'd pull me into the kitchen and take out a big bowl of fresh pasta she had made just for me.

As I grew up, moved away, and started my own family, I'd always return home for the holidays and eat a big bowl of my grandmother's pasta on Christmas. But in 2020, for the first time in my life, I didn't spend Christmas with my grandparents. My husband Steve and I had moved to North Carolina, and our daughter was only a few months old, so we weren't able to make the trip back to New York. I decided to make all the classic dishes we usually ate at Christmas—eggplant parm, ham, pies, cookies, and—of course—fresh pasta. It was just our little family, but it made me happy.

Two days after Christmas, my grandmother was unexpectedly rushed to the hospital. Steve and I made the long drive back to New York; by the time we arrived, she was back at her home but unconscious. Hospice workers set up a hospital bed in her living room, and for the next week my family gathered at her side day and night until she peacefully passed away in her sleep.

My grandmother was gone. My parental leave was ending, I was about to go back to work as a lawyer, and my daughter was not sleeping through the night. I can't quite explain why, but late at night I found myself drawn to the kitchen, clearing the counter, and making pasta. I suppose the meditative nature of kneading the dough helped me clear my mind, and the act of making pasta made me feel closer to my grandmother. I was making more than we could possibly eat, stocking my freezer with every new shape I attempted.

I started posting pasta-making videos on TikTok under the name Danny Loves Pasta as a way to document my progress. In my early videos, I kept it pretty traditional, turning classic pasta dough into classic pasta shapes like tortellini and ravioli, but every night after my daughter went to bed, I'd be back in the kitchen trying something new. I started incorporating spinach into my dough, and then beets, and then I realized I could use natural ingredients to make any color dough I wanted. I tried making different patterns and shapes, like striped farfalle and red roses. Soon, someone started commenting on all of my videos, asking me to make pasta out of Oreos. I dismissed this at first—Oreo pasta seemed a little too far out there for me—but then I thought *why not*; pasta doesn't have to have any rules! I made that Oreo pasta, and in that moment, @DannyLovesPasta was truly born.

I went on to make rainbow and animal print pasta, succulent ravioli and spiral lasagna, and pasta that looks like other foods, like cookies or watermelon. That's what I became known for, and that's what I want to teach you: how to make fresh pasta that is fun and whimsical, that brings a smile to your face and taps into your creative side. I hope to show you that making pasta can be joyful; by combining a

Taking a walk along Sunset Beach, NC, with my daughter.

My family, including our dog Bartley

few simple ingredients, you can make food that is both beautiful and delicious, and you can have a great time while doing so.

My approach to pasta is colorful and a little weird, but it's not all that difficult. With a bit of practice and a willingness to try new things, anyone can make bright, beautiful fresh pasta. You'll find all of the techniques I use in this book, but I hope you take what you learn here and make it all your own. Get creative—make your own patterns and colors, and see where your new pasta-making habit takes you!

Every once in a while, on some of my more outlandish videos, someone comments that their Italian ancestors would be horrified to see what I'm doing to pasta, or that their *nonna* would never approve. My grandmother didn't live to see my pasta-making journey, but I am 100 percent sure she would get the biggest kick out of what I'm doing, and she would absolutely love all of my pasta creations. Whatever you end up making from this book, I'm sure she would love yours, too. I can't wait to see what you come up with!

1

CHAPTER ONE

Equipment & Ingredients

When I was growing up, my parents would occasionally bring out my great-grandmother's pasta machine so we could make spaghetti. It didn't happen often, because it was an all-day affair that took over the house: We'd make a giant batch of dough and put sheets over the backs of all our chairs so we could lay out each strand of spaghetti, individually, to dry. My two brothers and I, and sometimes our friends from the neighborhood, would take turns cranking the pasta maker until invariably one of us would break it. The dough would clog up the decades-old machine, and my dad would have to pull it out of the narrow teeth of the spaghetti cutter. We'd lay each strand down carefully across the kitchen and living room, because they were usually pretty sticky; eventually, it seemed like spaghetti was everywhere. It always tasted great in the end, but it felt like a lot of work to get there.

Now that I make fresh pasta almost every day, I can't really take over the entire house when I do it. I mean, I wouldn't mind pasta everywhere, but my husband and daughter might start complaining. I also can't spend all day doing it; most days, I stay at home with my daughter, so if I want to be productive while making pasta, I have to do it during her nap time. That gives me roughly 90 minutes to make the dough, set up my tripod for filming, create the shape, cook it, clean up, edit the footage, come up with some sort of quippy caption, and post it to social media.

I've learned that having the right equipment and ingredients on hand is key for pasta making to be an easy and enjoyable experience. In this chapter, I lay out some of the most important tools I use to create the shapes and patterns in this book, as well as my recommendations for some commonly used ingredients. The best equipment, though, is the one you already own. Pasta making utilizes a lot of things you probably have in a kitchen drawer somewhere, like rolling pins, cookie cutters, and even cheese graters. There's nothing in this book that requires any expensive, special tools, so you're probably ready to start making pasta right now with the equipment you have on hand. If you plan on making this a hobby, this chapter gives advice on what to buy to make the process as easy as possible.

Equipment

Pasta making doesn't require much special equipment, and I can't imagine the Italian *nonne* of years ago were spending a fortune on fancy tools. In its simplest form, fresh pasta can be made with no equipment at all; all you need is two hands to knead the dough and roll it into *pici*, a rustic form of spaghetti. If you'd like to expand your repertoire, though, there are a few tools I'd recommend to make your life as a pasta chef easier. You probably have some of these lying around your kitchen already, and they are all readily available online.

Pasta Machine

If you're anything like me, there's probably been a time in your life when you got really excited about a new hobby and spent a bunch of money on special equipment, only to lose interest after a few weeks and leave everything to collect dust. Or, at the very least, you bought a new kitchen gadget that you just had to have, and now it's taking up precious space on your counter, hardly ever touched. So you might be wondering whether you *really* need a pasta machine, and I'm here to help you out.

First things first, there's not a single recipe in this book that requires a pasta machine. If you don't have one right now, don't let that stop you from diving in and getting started. The primary purpose of a pasta maker is to quickly roll the dough into a thin sheet, but you can produce the same results using a rolling pin (or even a wine bottle in a pinch). After all, pasta chefs survived for generations without ever needing an electric or mechanical tool to roll their dough, and many cooks today still prefer to roll their dough by hand.

That being said, a pasta machine will make the process much faster. What may otherwise take you twenty minutes and a bit of an arm workout can be done in seconds. If you plan on making pasta more than a couple of times, you'll likely appreciate having a machine roll the dough out for you. Most machines also include two cutters that quickly slice your dough into spaghetti or fettuccine, transforming fresh pasta making from an intimidating project to a delicious and easy meal you can have on the dinner table in no time.

If you are going to buy a pasta machine, there are three main types to choose from.

The first is the mechanical, hand-crank version that's been around forever. I have my great-grandmother's old pasta machine as well as one I bought recently, and truthfully they're not that different. They both clamp to your table or counter and have a crank that you turn to gradually roll the dough more thinly. The technology hasn't changed much in decades, because these pasta machines work so well. You can find them online or at most kitchen-supply stores at a relatively affordable price.

The second is an electric version of the hand-crank pasta machine. They look quite similar, but electric machines use a motor to roll the dough so you can give your arms a rest. They're quite a bit more expensive, but if you already have a hand-crank pasta machine and want to upgrade, some companies sell motors that attach to their machines and do the cranking for you.

Finally, if you have a KitchenAid mixer, you can buy attachments that use the machine's motor to roll out the dough. They are sold in a set of three attachments: one to roll the dough into a flat sheet and two others to cut the dough into spaghetti or fettuccine. This is the pasta maker that I use most frequently; I've been quite happy with it.

I should note that there is one more kind of pasta maker you may come across when doing your research, and that's the pasta extruder. These do not roll the dough into flat sheets but rather push it through little cut-outs to make shapes. They are smaller versions of the machines industrial pasta makers use to create all of the different shapes you can buy at the grocery store, but they aren't necessary to make the fresh pasta recipes you'll find in this book. They are a fun device but rather pricey; honestly, I haven't had great luck with the cheaper models.

Rolling Pin

If you don't have a pasta machine, you'll need a rolling pin to flatten the dough. Even with a pasta machine, I often use a rolling pin if I'm working on a delicate design or need to flatten some dough to help it fit into the machine. Any rolling pin will do, but if you want the most traditional option, you can buy a *mattarello*, an extra-long, perfectly smooth rolling pin used to make large sheets of pasta dough.

Pasta Wheel
(Also Called a Pastry Wheel)

After my pasta machine, this is the tool I use most often. It's a little circular knife on the end of a handle that you roll across a sheet of dough, allowing you to quickly and efficiently cut it into shapes. A regular knife works, too, but for long sheets of dough, it's much easier to use the rolling kind. You can get one with a jagged wheel, which is perfect for giving ravioli its characteristic edges. Or get a double-header, like the one I use, which has both a smooth and jagged wheel for either type of cut. If you're getting serious about pasta making, this is one tool I think it's worth spending a bit of extra money on. A cheaper rolling knife can snag and be frustrating, while a good-quality one glides across the dough effortlessly.

Multi-Blade Pastry Wheel

If you want to make your cutting job go a little faster, you can get a pastry wheel that cuts multiple lines into the dough at once. These tools have four to six evenly spaced blades that are either stationary or open up like an accordion. This allows you to cut the dough into perfect little squares or rectangles in no time.

X-Acto Knife

This may not be a traditional pasta-making tool, but it's a great one to have on hand when you're making some of the more intricate shapes in this book. It can sometimes be frustrating to try making precise cuts in the dough with a pasta wheel or even a regular knife, so sometimes an X-Acto knife is the best option.

Gnocchi Board

A gnocchi board (sometimes called a pasta board) is a piece of wood with grooves carved into it, and it's used to give gnocchi and other pasta shapes their characteristic ridges. The most common type has long vertical lines that give pasta a striped look, similar to the lines on penne or rigatoni, but you can find beautiful handmade boards online with all sorts of patterns. Many come with a small dowel, which you'll need to make several of the shapes in this book. If you don't have a gnocchi board (or its close cousin, a pasta comb), don't despair, as your pasta does not need to remain ridgeless. Many common kitchen tools can be used to create grooves in a piece of pasta, including a slotted spoon, the back of a fork, and a cheese grater.

Dough Scraper

A dough scraper (also called a bench scraper) is a handy tool often used for cutting, scooping, and moving dough. It's basically a flat rectangle with a dull edge, and I use one every time I'm making pasta. When combining the flour and eggs to make dough, the mixture will eventually become too thick to stir with a fork; at this point, I use my dough scraper to continue bringing the ingredients together. It's also quite useful for scraping up the little bits of dough that stick to the counter once you're done. It's certainly not necessary, but if you have one already, you should break it out.

Cookie Cutters

Cookie cutters are some of the best pasta tools you can own: They're readily available, they come in endless shapes, and there's a good chance you already have a few at home. I use them quite a bit to make ravioli or patterned pasta, and any of your favorite shapes or designs will do. I especially recommend getting a set of circular cookie cutters, as many traditional pasta shapes start with circles of varying sizes. You can also use the top of a wine glass or other cup with a decently sharp edge, but cookie cutters will definitely be easier. If you'd like to be a little more traditional, you can get a few ravioli stamps, which are heftier and usually have jagged edges.

Plunger Cutters

In addition to regular cookie cutters, I often use plunger cutters, which are smaller and used primarily for cake decorating. You can use them to make little polka dots, stars, or other shapes for some beautiful patterned pasta.

Piping Bags

Whenever I'm making ravioli, I use a piping bag to add my filling to the pasta. You can use a spoon, of course, but a piping bag gives you better control over how much filling you're adding and where. When you're getting into more complicated shapes and need to place the filling in a line, a circle, or the outline of a flower, a piping bag is a big help.

Spray Bottle

Pasta dough dries out quickly and will start to crack when you bend it. To counteract this, I always keep a spray bottle on hand to give the dough a light mist of water whenever it's too dry and needs to be a little more pliable.

Kitchen Scale

When making pasta dough, I always weigh the flour with a kitchen scale rather than measuring by volume. There's no standard weight for 1 cup of flour and it can vary by brand and type of flour. Although I've given an estimate for how much flour to use by volume in each of these recipes, you'll get the most accurate results if you measure by weight.

Ingredients

Most of the ingredients in this book don't need much explanation, as I generally use common vegetables and spices to add color to the pasta doughs and flavor to the sauces. However, there are a few that could use a bit of clarification. While this is definitely not an exhaustive list of the ingredients in this book, it will hopefully provide you with a bit more information on what to look for when you're grocery shopping.

Flour

Flour forms the basis of pretty much every type of pasta, whether dry or fresh, so it's important to have a good understanding of it. I generally use six or seven types of flour when making pasta, but I promise you it's not as complicated as it sounds, and I'll explain each one here.

- **00 flour** (sometimes labeled Double-Zero) is a soft wheat flour that's more finely ground than all-purpose flour, meaning it's great for creating soft and supple doughs. Traditionally, fresh pasta is made entirely with 00 flour. In the United States, we generally categorize flours based on protein levels, which is why cake flour is different than bread flour, which is different than all-purpose flour. Italy adds another classification system based on how finely ground the flour is, so flour can be labeled 00, 0, 1, or 2. Technically, "double-zero" refers only to how finely ground the flour is, and any type of flour can be ground to double-zero. But if you see a flour labeled "double-zero," "00," or "pasta flour," it's most likely the right stuff for pasta making. My preferred flour brand is Antimo Caputo, but I also like Anna Tipo 00 and Molino

Grassi. I've found them all online and at specialty grocery stores.

- **Semola flour** is made from durum wheat, the same type of wheat that's used to make boxed pasta. It has a higher protein level than all-purpose flour, which helps dry pasta keep its shape when it's cooked. For this reason, I include semola flour in my pasta dough recipe; while it's not necessary if you're just cutting the dough into spaghetti or fettuccine, it helps keep the dough sturdy for more complicated shapes. It's easy to confuse semola with the next flour on this list, semolina, and while they're quite similar, they're not exactly the same. Semola is a more finely ground version of semolina; I prefer to use it in my dough because it more closely matches the texture of 00 flour, whereas semolina can be quite coarse and grainy. My preferred brand is Caputo Semola Rimacinata, which I've seen at some grocery stores but is more widely available online.

- **Semolina flour** is the third type of flour I always keep on hand. Because it's so coarse, I don't usually put it in my dough, but it's my go-to choice for dusting sticky surfaces. I dust it on my dough as I'm rolling it through my pasta maker, I put some on my cutting board before shaping, and I sprinkle a lot on my pasta before cooking so the pieces don't stick to each other. Since semolina is so coarse, it tends to sit on the surface of the dough rather than dissolve into it. It's much easier to find than semola, so if it's all you can get, it's fine to use it in the dough as well. I like Bob's Red Mill Semolina because it's widely available and isn't too expensive.

- **All-purpose flour** is the flour you probably already have in your pantry. Although my Classic Pasta Dough (page 38) uses 00 flour and semola, it's perfectly fine to use all-purpose if that's what you have on hand, and I use it quite often when I've run out of the other two.

- **Gluten-free flours** can be made from many different ingredients, from rice to almonds to chickpeas to hazelnuts to corn. You can experiment with any of them when making pasta, but you'll likely need to use a thickening agent like xanthan gum to give the pasta a chewy feel. My Gluten-Free Pasta Dough (page 44) uses a rice flour mix as its base (I'm partial to King Arthur Gluten Free All-Purpose Flour or King Arthur Gluten Free Measure for Measure Flour) along with chickpea flour and tapioca flour.

Eggs

Eggs are the other main ingredient in fresh pasta. All the recipes in this book use large eggs, so if you use a smaller egg, you may need to add a little bit of water to the dough to get the texture right. A large egg should weigh about 50 grams (1.7 ounces) without the shell, with the yolk weighing about 20 grams (0.7 ounces). If you're unsure if your eggs are the right size, you can weigh them to be safe.

Salt

Salt plays an important role in nearly all the recipes in this book. I always add salt to the water when boiling pasta, and I use it in most of the sauces. The purpose of adding salt is not to make the food taste salty; rather, it helps enhance the natural flavors of the ingredients. Most of the recipes call for adding a bit of salt at the beginning, tasting the sauce as it's cooking, and then adding more salt if necessary. I've left the exact amount of salt imprecise on purpose, because you really need to be tasting the sauce throughout the cooking process and deciding if it needs more salt. If you taste the sauce and it feels like it's missing something, or it's just a little bit flat, there's a good chance it needs more salt. If you're not sure, add a little bit at a time, stir it in, and then taste the sauce again. I use Diamond Crystal kosher salt, and although some chefs are sticklers about it, I think it's fine to use whatever salt you have on hand. Be aware, though, that different salt types actually have different sodium levels by volume, so a teaspoon of fine table salt will be a lot saltier than a teaspoon of coarse kosher salt.

Parmigiano Reggiano and Pecorino Romano

Many of the sauce recipes call for grated cheese, either mixed into the sauce itself or sprinkled on the pasta at the end. Parmigiano Reggiano is a hard cheese with a mild, nutty flavor made from cow's milk, while Pecorino Romano comes from sheep's milk and has a saltier, tangier taste. Parmigiano Reggiano is often referred to as "Parmesan" and that's the term I use throughout this book, but it's important to note the differences between these two names. Authentic Parmigiano Reggiano is strictly regulated by the Italian government and aged for at least a year, whereas anything can be labeled Parmesan. For the best quality, I recommend looking for one labeled Parmigiano Reggiano or that has a DOP (protected designation of origin) seal on it. In a pinch, it's fine to use either Parmesan or Pecorino for the recipes in this book, but I tend to use Parmesan in my sauces because it has a mellower flavor. In either case, it's best to buy a block of cheese and grate it yourself for the freshest taste. When it comes to which cheese to sprinkle on top of your pasta after it's cooked, it's totally up to you. A lot of restaurants serve Parmesan for that purpose, but I come from a Pecorino family.

Tomatoes

Several of the sauce recipes in this book use tomatoes as one of the main ingredients, and while you may be able to get some tasty fresh ones in the summer, I use canned tomatoes all year round. The key is to look for San Marzano or San Marzano–style tomatoes. They're a type of plum tomato traditionally grown in the San Marzano region of Southern Italy, and they're known for their sweet, rich flavor. Authentic tomatoes grown in San Marzano and meeting strict qualifications will have a DOP seal on them, but they can be rather pricey. I've had good luck with less expensive varieties grown in the U.S., so look for ones labeled "San Marzano Style" or "Italian Style." I almost always use whole tomatoes rather than crushed as these have the best flavor, and I crush them by hand or blend them.

2

CHAPTER TWO

Doughs

When my grandmother turned 90, we threw a big birthday party for her. All her children and grandchildren were there, along with cousins, nieces, and nephews, and all their spouses. After we'd all had more than enough to eat, someone gave a toast, and then there was another. This being a big group of Italian Americans, there were plenty of interruptions, a lot of wisecracking, a few lighthearted jokes at the youngest cousin's expense, and someone shouting out a *Godfather* reference about kissing the ring (really, I have the speech recorded). Then, finally, my grandmother decided to say a few words herself. She looked around at all of us gathered and said, "This is what's important in life: family. I've had good times in life, and sickness, but I've always had family, and nothing beats that. Money, eh, but family—always remember family."

Family was a common theme of my grandmother's toasts, as she often talked about how lucky she was to have her family together for holidays and birthdays. Family didn't just mean the one you're born into or the people you share DNA with. It's the people you laugh with late into the night long after the plates have been cleared, and the ones you call when life feels overwhelming. More than anything, family is the people who are there for you, the ones who show up when you need them most and who stand by your side when it feels like no one else will.

When my grandmother passed away, I wrote a long eulogy to read at her funeral, scribbling down words on a piece of paper in a desperate attempt to try to explain what she meant to me. It was a hopeless task, really, because no words would ever be adequate. When I got up at the front of the church, I could hardly speak a word. I was on the verge of bursting into tears, and reading the eulogy felt nearly impossible. I had written down my grandmother's speech from her 90th birthday, because the message felt truer than ever. And that's all I was able to get out: "This is what's important in life: family. Always remember family."

Making fresh pasta by hand is the perfect embodiment of what family means to me. It's truly an act of love: folding and kneading simple ingredients until they turn into something magical. It feels joyful and fun, and it's a way to nourish your body and fill you with energy. This chapter teaches you how to make a variety of pasta doughs by hand—classic, vegan, gluten-free—and even includes a gnocchi recipe. The process is similar for all of them, using techniques that have been around for generations. My hope is that you'll enjoy the experience as much as I do, and that making fresh pasta will become so much more than simply having something to eat.

How to Make Pasta Dough: The Basics

Every time I serve someone a bowl of fresh pasta, I have a moment of doubt. I don't worry about whether they'll like it or not—after all, who doesn't like pasta?—but I imagine them thinking *What's all the fuss? Why does he spend all that time making this when he could just pour a box into boiling water like everyone else?* And then I take a bite, and immediately relax, and remember that I have nothing to worry about. There's something indescribably seductive about fresh pasta, like an abstract painting that doesn't look like much at first yet you can't stop staring at it. It's simple—just a few ingredients—but after you take one bite, all you want to do is take another one. Fresh pasta, especially when paired with the perfect sauce, is the type of dish you go back to for seconds, and then thirds. It draws you in, and with each bite you'll fall in love with it more and more.

This section forms the basis for all the recipes in this book, so if you can master my Classic Pasta Dough (page 38), you're well on your way to becoming a pasta artist. I'll go into the most detail here, so refer back to these steps later on when you're adding color to your dough in chapter 3.

Combining Your Flour and Eggs

My Classic Pasta Dough recipe (page 38) calls for 250 grams (1¾ cups) of double-zero flour, 150 grams (¾ cup) of semola flour, and 4 large eggs. Start by combining the flours in a pile on your kitchen counter, table, or other flat work surface. Or, if you prefer a less messy version, place them all in a large mixing bowl.

Next, use the bottom of a medium bowl or your hands to make a deep indentation in the middle of the pile of flour. Crack your eggs into the well in the flour and use a fork to scramble the yolks and the whites together. As you're mixing, scrape the bottom of the pile to pull in a little bit of flour at a time. Keep scrambling the eggs until most of the flour lumps are gone. Then slowly drag in a little more flour from the sides of the well, mixing it with the eggs for a few seconds to incorporate.

Continue dragging in the flour and mixing it with the eggs until the mixture is too thick to mix with a fork. At this point, I like to use a dough scraper, but a spatula or even your hands will work as well. Pull up the flour on the outskirts of your pile and press it into the eggy center. You'll feel that some parts of the dough are very floury and some are very liquidy—that just means you need to keep going. Keep combining the flour and eggs until there are no more obvious wet spots left and you mostly see clumps of flour.

Now start using your hands if you haven't already—get in there and start bringing all the clumps together. You should be able to form a very loose ball of dough. It won't be perfect, and there will be little bits of flour that keep falling off, but at this point you should be able to combine most of the dough together into one mass.

Getting the Moisture Content Right

This is the most important part of making pasta dough, so read this part carefully. Almost every day someone sends me a message telling me they tried to make fresh pasta but it came out really sticky or slimy, or it all clumped together when

they cooked it, or they ended up with a giant mess of gluey, mushy pasta. That's because the moisture content was off, and now is the time to get it right.

There are many factors that affect the moisture content of your dough, and even if you've followed the recipe precisely, you still might have to make adjustments. Your eggs may be different sizes, your flour might be more or less absorbent, or there might be some water remaining on your hands after washing them. Even the humidity in the air can impact the feel of your dough. It sounds complicated, but the solution is quite simple, and before too long, adjusting the moisture content of your dough will become second nature.

If, after you've combined the flour and the eggs, the mixture feels really crumbly and is just not coming together into a dough ball, you'll need to add a little water. Start slowly, adding just a spoonful at a time, and see if that helps. Work the moisture into the dough with your hands until most of the dough comes together into a ball.

On the flip side, if the dough feels slimy and is sticking to your hands or your workspace after you've formed it into a ball, it needs a little more flour. Sprinkle on a big pinch of flour and work it into the dough to see if it helps.

You may need to adjust several times, adding a little bit of flour or a little bit of water until you get it right. You should be able to form a fairly cohesive ball of dough, but the dough should not be sticking to your hands or feel wet at this point.

Kneading the Dough

Once you have a loose ball of dough, clear out all the little pieces of flour and egg that are remaining on your work surface and wash the sticky bits off your hands. Start kneading the dough by pressing into the dough with the heel of your hand, folding the dough onto itself, and then pressing some more. Rotate the dough and repeat the folding and pressing action. It's not too late to get the moisture content right: If the dough is sticking to your hands or the surface, sprinkle on a little more flour and incorporate it.

Knead the dough for about 5 minutes until the texture starts to change. It should feel smoother, with the dough softening and becoming easier to knead. Cover your dough with an airtight bowl or wrap it in plastic and let it rest for about 10 minutes (if you're pressed for time, you can skip this step). The initial resting period helps the gluten structures develop, giving your pasta that characteristic chewy bite.

After the dough has rested, knead it for about 3 more minutes. You should now be able to form a ball with a nice smooth top and no visible pieces of flour. Wrap it up again and leave it for a second resting period, this time for at least 1 hour. Once it's rested, you're ready to start shaping.

If you're not ready to start working, you can refrigerate the dough for up to 24 hours. Take the dough out of the fridge at least 30 minutes before you plan to use it, so it has time to come to room temperature.

Dividing the Dough

Some of the recipes in this book call for using a half batch or quarter batch of pasta dough. If you're making less than a full batch of dough, keep this ratio in mind: 1 egg per 100 grams of flour. My Classic Pasta Dough (page 38) uses 400 grams of flour. To make half a batch, use 2 eggs and 200 grams of flour. To make a quarter batch, use 1 egg and 100 grams of flour. Since most of my recipes use both 00 and semola flours, here are the ratios I use if I'm not making a full batch of dough:

- **Half batch:** 2 large eggs, 125 g (¾ cup) 00 flour, 75 g (½ cup) semola flour

- **Quarter batch:** 1 large egg, 60 g (¼ cup plus 2 tablespoons) 00 flour, 40 g (¼ cup) semola flour

Working with Fresh Pasta Dough

Once your dough has rested, you're ready to start shaping! No matter what shape you're making, the first step almost always involves rolling your dough into a flat sheet of pasta.

Rolling by Hand

If you're rolling your dough by hand, there's a beautiful, traditional method you can learn to create a *sfoglia*: the large, flat, circular sheet of dough that Bolognese pasta makers use when making pasta. When I'm rolling pasta dough by hand, I don't bother with this method because I think there's an easier way to do it (hopefully none of my Italian ancestors are looking down at me right now and frowning). If you really want to become a *sfoglina*, I suggest watching some videos online to learn this technique.

For my method, you'll start with your ball of dough, cut it into quarters, and then work with one piece at a time. Dust some flour on a smooth work surface (a wooden table or board works best) and

start rolling your dough with a large rolling pin into a loose rectangular shape. It's going to take some elbow grease, so keep rolling. Most of the recipes in this book call for you to roll the dough to about 1 millimeter thick (for shapes like ravioli, which has multiple layers, you'll want to roll it even thinner). It helps to drape some of the dough over the edge of your counter or workspace, which will hold your dough in place, and then use a lot of force to roll the remaining dough on the counter away from you.

You don't have to worry about making a perfect shape with the dough (remember, you're going to be cutting it up anyway!); it's okay if it doesn't look pretty. Your goal is to make an even, thin sheet of pasta with no tears and no big lumps. Remember that it's harder to roll out dough by hand if it has a lot of semola flour in it, since semola has a higher protein level, so if you're going to be doing a lot of hand rolling, I would suggest using a dough made of all double-zero flour.

Using a Pasta Machine

You don't need a pasta machine to make any of the recipes in this book, but it certainly helps make the process a little faster and easier (okay, a lot faster and easier). That's because the machine will do all the rolling for you, and if you're making shapes like fettuccine or spaghetti, the machine will cut the dough for you, too. Regardless of what shape you're making, here are a few tips and tricks you should know.

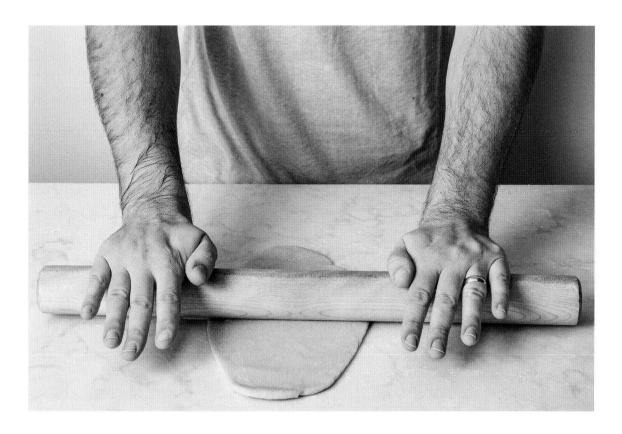

Start by cutting your ball of dough into quarters and working with one piece at a time, leaving the remaining dough covered so it doesn't dry out. Use your hand or a rolling pin to flatten the dough to about half an inch thick and dust each side with a little bit of flour. Then feed the dough through the widest setting on your pasta machine.

The dough should roll through the machine smoothly, but sometimes it comes out in thin stringy pieces, almost as if it's been shredded and ripped apart. There are three main reasons this can happen.

First, the dough might be too cold. If you left your dough in the fridge before rolling it out, you'll need to bring it to room temperature first.

Second, you might be trying to stuff too much dough into the machine at once, and you'll need to flatten it first.

And third, the gluten structures might not have formed properly, and you'll need to laminate the dough more (see below).

No matter the reason, this problem is easily fixed: Pick up all the pieces, stack them on top of each other, and keep running the dough through your machine until it's smooth.

Laminating the Dough

Once you've rolled the dough through the widest setting on your pasta machine, you'll need to laminate it. Pasta's nice, chewy texture that we all know and love is thanks to the gluten structures inside, and we have to work to develop that gluten. There are three ways to do this: by kneading the dough, by letting it rest, and by laminating it. If you're in a rush and had to skip the resting phase,

it's especially important that you laminate the dough, but you should do it every time you make pasta dough, no matter what.

Okay, so what *is* laminating? It's the process of folding the dough onto itself and then running it through the machine over and over, almost like a machine-powered version of kneading. After you've run your dough through the machine once, fold the dough into thirds as if you were folding a piece of paper to place it in an envelope. Then run the pasta through the machine again at the same setting, putting one of the short ends of the dough through first. Fold the dough into thirds and run it through the machine again at the widest setting. Repeat this process three to four times, and you're ready to proceed.

Turn your pasta machine to the next thinnest setting and run the dough through again. You may need to dust the dough with some extra flour, especially if it's moist or sticking. If at any point you notice the dough tearing or bubbling up, you'll need to sprinkle on some more flour and run it through again. Keep running the dough through the machine, changing the setting to be thinner each time, until you've reached your desired thickness.

Adding Moisture

After you've rolled out your pasta dough, place it on a piece of parchment paper or a floured surface so it doesn't stick. Cover the dough with a slightly dampened kitchen towel so it doesn't dry out while you're shaping your pasta. If it does start to dry out and becomes difficult to work with, spray the dough with a very small amount of water from a spray bottle or use a brush or paper towel to lightly brush on some water.

Cooking Fresh Pasta

Once you've cut your pasta into whatever beautiful shape you've chosen, let it sit out for about 10 minutes and then you're ready to cook it. It's fine if it sits out longer than that while you work, but there's no need to let it fully dry before throwing it into some boiling water. If you're able to cook a box of pasta, I'm confident you'll be able to handle fresh pasta, but here are a few tips to keep in mind:

- Use enough water so that your pasta has room to move around. If you don't use enough water, the pasta will end up clumping together. For a pound of pasta, that means at least 4 quarts (3.75 L) of water.

- Unless you have a dietary restriction, cook your pasta in salted water. This is not to make the pasta taste salty, but rather to enhance its natural flavor. You should use enough salt to make the water taste like mild seawater; for 4 quarts (3.75 L) of water, that's 1½ to 2 tablespoons of salt. Of course, you're free to add more or less according to your preference.

- Some people say you should add salt at the very beginning, because it helps the water boil faster. Others will tell you that's wrong—it actually slows down the boiling process—and the proper method is to wait until the water is boiling, add salt, let it come back to a boil, and then add your pasta. Hopefully I don't get in trouble for saying this, but I'm here to tell you that it doesn't really matter when you add the salt. I've tried both ways, and if there's any difference in cooking time, it's minimal. I prefer to add the salt at the beginning when the water is still cold; that way you can taste the water to see if it's salty enough without burning your tongue!

- Fresh pasta cooks much more quickly than dry pasta, so don't leave your pasta cooking for 10 minutes and expect it to turn out fine. The cooking time will depend on how thinly you've rolled the dough, but it's usually somewhere in the range of 2 to 6 minutes. If you've rolled the dough to the thinnest setting on a pasta machine (less than a millimeter thick), it should cook in 3 minutes tops. If your pasta is thicker or has a lot of folds, it will take longer. If you cook your pasta straight from the freezer, it will take an extra minute. My best advice is to keep tasting the pasta every minute or so until you develop a good sense of how long it takes to cook.

Storing Fresh Pasta

If you don't want to cook all your pasta at once, you have three main options for storage: drying, refrigerating, and freezing. I'm a strong proponent of freezing over the other two methods, but I'll give you instructions for each so you can decide what works best for you.

Drying

Once you've shaped your pasta, leave it out overnight on a piece of parchment paper or a floured surface where it won't stick. Make sure that the pieces are separated so they don't clump together. If you are making long noodles, like tagliatelle, you can hang them on a wooden pasta rack, if you have one, or you can make your own with a long dowel or a few clothes hangers. After they've dried, carefully move the pasta to an airtight bag until you're ready to cook. They should last about a week, though if there are vegetables mixed in with the dough, they may only last a few days before they start to mold. Drying can make the pasta very brittle, especially if it's been rolled thin, so handle it carefully! And one final note: Please don't try this method with ravioli. You don't want to eat a cheese filling that's been sitting out on your counter all week!

Refrigerating

This is the easiest method if you plan on eating the pasta within a day or so. After it's cut, place it on a tray lined with parchment paper or flour, making sure the individual pieces aren't touching each other, and stick it in the fridge. It should last for 24 hours, and you can take it right out of the fridge to cook. I don't recommend refrigerating ravioli, even if you're going to eat them in a few hours, because the filling will seep through the dough and make the pasta soggy.

Freezing

This is my preferred method for pasta storage. Whenever I'm not going to eat the pasta within a few hours, I pop it in the freezer. Place a sheet of parchment paper on a cookie sheet or cutting board and lay each piece of pasta individually so they're not touching. For ravioli, I also lay down a thick layer of flour. Place them in the freezer; after about an hour, they should be frozen and you can transfer them to a freezer-safe bag or container—at this point, you don't have to worry about them touching since they're already frozen, so feel free to fill your bag to save space! They should last in the freezer for about a month, and you can throw them right from the freezer into boiling water when you're ready to cook. Because they're frozen, you may need to add a minute or so to the cooking time, but other than that, you can cook them like normal.

Classic Pasta Dough

PREP TIME 20 MIN, PLUS 1 HR REST TIME | 4 to 6 SERVINGS

This recipe forms the basis for all of the others in this book, but it absolutely holds up on its own. Once you learn how to make this dough, you can whip it up on a weeknight and pair it with your favorite sauce for a quick dinner. It can be made ahead of time or at the last minute (if you're in a time crunch, you can skip the hourlong resting period, but check out the section on laminating your dough on page 35). After a few attempts, the whole process will become second nature, and you'll soon become your own version of an Italian nonna, instinctively knowing just how the dough should feel to get that perfect, chewy bite.

250 g (1¾ cups) 00 flour

150 g (¾ cup) semola flour

4 large eggs

1. Combine the flours in a pile on a flat work surface or in a large bowl. Make a deep well in the middle.

2. Crack the eggs into the well and use a fork to scramble them. Pull in a little bit of flour from the bottom of the well and mix it with the eggs until most of the lumps are gone.

3. Drag in flour from the edges of your well and incorporate with the eggs. Keep incorporating more and more of the flour and eggs until the mixture becomes difficult to stir with a fork.

4. Using a dough scraper, a spatula, or your hands, continue combining the flour with the eggs until no liquid remains. Use your hands to bring the dough together into a loose ball.

5. If the dough is very crumbly and doesn't come together, add a spoonful of water. If it's very slimy, incorporate a spoonful of 00 flour. You may need to do this several times to get it right—most of the dough should be coming together into a ball, but it shouldn't be sticking to your hands at this point.

6. Remove any remaining bits of flour stuck to your work surface or hands and knead the dough for about 5 minutes, until the texture starts to change and becomes smooth.

7. Wrap the dough in plastic wrap or cover with an airtight bowl and let rest for 10 minutes. Then knead again for about 3 minutes, until you have a fairly smooth ball.

8. Cover or wrap the dough again and let rest for at least 1 hour.

ALL-OO CLASSIC PASTA DOUGH

To make a dough that's easier to roll out by hand, leave out the semola flour and use 400 g (2¾ cups) 00 flour.

WHOLE WHEAT CLASSIC PASTA DOUGH

To make a whole wheat dough with a sandy brown color, use 400 grams (2¾ cups) of whole wheat flour instead of the 00 and semola flours.

PASTA HISTORY

There's a persistent myth that Marco Polo first brought pasta to Italy from China in the 13th century, but it certainly existed in the region long before then. Some historians believe that a 400 BCE Etruscan tomb from Tuscany depicts rudimentary pasta-making tools, while others believe Arab traders first brought pasta using durum wheat to Sicily in the 9th century.

Food Processor Pasta Dough

PREP TIME 5 MIN, PLUS 1 HR REST TIME | 4 to 6 SERVINGS

There's something beautiful, even meditative, about making pasta dough the old-fashioned way, with the mixing and the combining and the kneading. You're connected to the generations of pasta makers who have come before you, and if you close your eyes and stretch your imagination, you can almost picture yourself in the Italian countryside. But sometimes modern technology comes in handy, and this method will give you fresh pasta dough in just a few minutes without the arm workout. You can skip the resting period if you're in a hurry, but check out the section on laminating your dough on page 35 if you do so.

250 g (1¾ cups) 00 flour

150 g (¾ cup) semola flour

4 large eggs

1. Place the ingredients in a food processor and run the machine on high for about 20 seconds.

2. Take a look inside: You should see tiny pebbles of dough that look almost like couscous. If the mixture looks slimy and watery, add a spoonful of 00 flour and run the food processor for another 20 seconds. If the dough feels very dry and floury, add a small spoonful of water.

3. Run the machine for another 30 seconds until the dough has started to clump together. It may become difficult for the food processor to run because the dough is clogging up the blade; that's a good sign that it's done.

4. Remove the dough and any remaining dough pebbles from the food processor and knead for a minute or so until it comes together in one smooth ball.

5. Cover the dough with an airtight bowl or wrap in plastic and let rest for 1 hour before shaping.

NOTE

Nearly all the dough recipes in this book will work in a food processor. If you're using a powder like turmeric or paprika, just add a spoonful to the food processor along with the flour and eggs. If you're incorporating vegetables into your dough, I recommend pureeing them first with the eggs and then adding them to the flour in the food processor.

Vegan Pasta Dough

PREP TIME 20 MIN, PLUS 1 HR REST TIME | 4 to 6 SERVINGS

You may see the word *vegan* and be tempted to skip this page. But I hope you'll stick around to learn this classic recipe; it contains just flour and water, all you need to make amazing pasta. This is the dough Italians have been using for generations to make Cavatelli (page 117), little hand-formed pillowy bites of pasta goodness. You can also make this recipe exclusively with semolina flour, which will give you the perfect dough to make orecchiette, another classic shape. While not as rich as an egg pasta, this dough proves that simple ingredients can make amazing food. It won't have enough structure for some of the intricate shapes in this book, but it does quite well as Farfalle (page 107) or fettuccine.

250 g (1¾ cups) 00 flour

150 g (¾ cup) semola flour

175 ml (¾ cup) water

1. Combine the flours in a pile on a flat work surface or in a large bowl. Make a deep well in the middle. To prevent the water from spilling all over your surface, make sure the flour pile is very tall and the well is very deep.

2. Pour the water into the middle of the well and use a fork to pull in a little bit of flour from the bottom of your well, slowly, to prevent splashing. Mix until most of the lumps are gone and a thick paste forms.

3. Drag in more flour from the edges of your well and incorporate with the water. Keep incorporating until the mixture becomes difficult to stir with a fork.

4. Using a dough scraper, a spatula, or your hands, continue combining the flour with the water until no liquid remains. Use your hands to bring the dough together into a loose ball.

5. If the dough is very crumbly and does not come together, add a spoonful of water. If it's very slimy, incorporate a spoonful of additional 00 flour. You may need to do this several times to get it right—most of the dough should be coming together into one ball, but it shouldn't be sticking to your hands at this point.

6. Remove any remaining bits of flour stuck to your work surface and knead the dough for about 5 minutes, until the texture starts to change and becomes smooth.

7. Wrap the dough in plastic wrap or cover with an airtight bowl and let rest for 10 minutes. Then knead again for about 3 minutes to form a fairly smooth ball of dough.

8. Cover or wrap the dough again and let rest for at least 1 hour.

PASTA HISTORY

Although pasta is now synonymous with Italian cuisine, people all over the world have been combining flour with water to make noodles for centuries. There's evidence that some form of noodle existed in China during the Shang Dynasty between 1700 and 1100 BCE, and ancient Greek texts speak of *laganon*, a precursor to lasagna.

ALL-00 VEGAN DOUGH

To make a vegan dough that's easier to roll out by hand, leave out the semola flour and use 400 g (2¾ cups) 00 flour.

All-Yolk Pasta Dough

PREP TIME 20 MIN, PLUS 1 HR REST TIME | 2 to 4 SERVINGS

Some pasta makers prefer to use only yolks when making their dough. This gives the pasta a richer taste and smoother texture, with a beautiful deep yellow color. The dough won't have as much structure or sturdiness as the Classic Pasta Dough (page 38), however, so it's a bit difficult to work with when making more intricate shapes. I prefer to use all-yolk dough for shapes that are rolled out flat, like Tagliatelle (page 102) or Ravioli (page 122), rather than shapes with a lot of bends and folds. This recipe assumes each yolk weighs 20 grams (0.7 ounces)—the standard size for a large egg—but if your yolks are smaller, you may need to add a spoonful or two of water.

275 g (2 cups) 00 flour, plus more for dusting

12 egg yolks

1. Place the flour in a pile on a flat work surface or in a large bowl. Make a deep well in the middle.

2. Pour the yolks into the well and use a fork to scramble them. Pull in a little bit of flour from the bottom of your well and mix it with the yolks until most of the lumps are gone.

3. Drag in flour from the edges of your well and incorporate with the yolks. Keep incorporating until the mixture becomes difficult to stir with a fork.

4. Using a dough scraper, a spatula, or your hands, continue combining the flour with the eggs until no liquid remains. Use your hands to bring the dough together into a loose ball.

5. If the dough is very crumbly and does not come together, add a spoonful of water. If it's very slimy, incorporate a spoonful of additional flour. You may need to do this several times to get it right—most of the dough should be coming together into one ball, but it shouldn't be sticking to your hands at this point.

6. Remove any remaining bits of flour stuck to your work surface and knead the dough for about 5 minutes, until the texture starts to change and becomes smooth.

7. Wrap the dough in plastic wrap or cover with an airtight bowl and let rest for 10 minutes. Then knead it again for about 3 minutes to form a fairly smooth ball of dough.

8. Cover or wrap the dough again and let rest for at least 1 hour.

PASTA HISTORY

For many generations, fresh pasta was made with only flour and water, since eggs were an expensive ingredient that couldn't be purchased on a regular basis. As a result, egg pasta was often reserved for holidays and special occasions. *Anolini*, for example, is a meat-filled ravioli made with an egg dough that is often served at Christmas in the northern Italian city of Parma. Similarly, *pincarelle* was a thick, hand-formed spaghetti frequently made by nuns in the province of Rieti, near Rome. A version made with egg dough was commonly given as Christmas gifts throughout the area.

Gluten-Free Pasta Dough

PREP TIME 20 MIN | 4 to 6 SERVINGS

If you spend any time searching online for gluten-free pasta recipes, you'll find plenty making this bold claim: "My spouse/friends/children couldn't even tell it was gluten-free!" I'm not going to make that claim, because I tried every one of those gluten-free recipes and, well, I could always tell. Gluten gives traditional pasta its characteristic stretchy, tender bite; to approximate that in my gluten-free dough, I've added two thickeners: xanthan gum and tapioca flour. To add some flavor, I've incorporated a few extra egg yolks, olive oil, and salt. The result is a gluten-free flour that doesn't fall apart, cooks well, and tastes great. Note that, without gluten, it's difficult to make some of the more intricate shapes in this book, so I recommend sticking to a relatively flat noodle like Tagliatelle (page 102) or Farfalle (page 107).

240 g (1½ cups) gluten-free flour mix (see Tip 1)

60 g (½ cup) chickpea flour

45 g (⅓ cup) tapioca flour (also called tapioca starch)

1 teaspoon xanthan gum (see Tip 2)

1 teaspoon salt

3 large eggs

3 egg yolks

1½ teaspoons olive oil

1. Mix the flours, xanthan gum, and salt in a pile on a flat work surface or in a large bowl. Make a deep well in the middle.

2. Combine the eggs, yolks, and olive oil in a bowl, then pour the mixture into the well. Use a fork to pull in a little bit of flour from the bottom. Mix with the eggs until most of the lumps are gone.

3. Drag in flour from the edges of your well and incorporate with the eggs. Keep incorporating more and more of the flour and eggs until the mixture becomes difficult to stir with a fork.

4. Using a dough scraper, a spatula, or your hands, continue combining the flour with the eggs until no liquid remains. Use your hands to bring the dough together into a loose ball.

5. If the dough is very crumbly and does not come together, add a spoonful of water. If it's very slimy, dust on additional gluten-free flour. You may need to do this several times to get it right—most of the dough should be coming together into one ball, but it shouldn't be sticking to your hands at this point.

6. Knead the dough for about 1 minute to form a smooth ball. Since we're not trying to develop any gluten, you don't need to worry about kneading the dough for very long, but you do want to make sure the flour and eggs are fully combined.

7. There's no need to let this dough rest, so it's ready to work with right away.

TIPS

1. Look for flours labeled "gluten-free all-purpose flour" or as a one-to-one substitute for wheat flour.

2. If your flour already contains xanthan gum, only add ¼ teaspoon.

3. If you're running the dough through a pasta machine, make sure it's very flat before you begin. Since this dough won't have the stretchiness of regular dough, it will tear into pieces if you try to put too much through the machine. If that happens, smush the pieces together, flatten them, and run the dough through the machine again.

Sweet Potato Gnocchi

PREP TIME 20 MIN | 4 to 6 SERVINGS

Some people might not consider gnocchi a type of pasta, but I hope we can all agree that at the very least it's a close cousin. Or perhaps an ancestor, since gnocchi has been around a lot longer than many of the shapes we know and love today. Early gnocchi were made of just flour and water; today, they can be made with many different vegetables—peas, beets, kale, squash—but here I go with sweet potatoes, a slight twist on the classic.

2 medium sweet potatoes (about 450 g/1 pound)

130 g (½ cup) ricotta

30 g (¼ cup) grated Parmesan

1 egg yolk

1 teaspoon salt, plus more for the pasta water

½ teaspoon freshly ground black pepper

250 g (1¾ cups) 00 flour, divided, plus more for dusting

PASTA HISTORY
The Italian city of Verona celebrates Gnocchi Friday on the final Friday before Lent. The tradition dates back to 1531, when the area was facing a food shortage and wealthy citizens provided flour so their poorer neighbors could make gnocchi. Today it's celebrated with a parade led by Papà del Gnoco (Gnocchi's Dad), a man with a red cape, bushy white beard, and large scepter in the shape of a fork with a giant gnocchi on it.

1. Pierce the sweet potatoes with a fork several times.

2. Cook the potatoes in the microwave on high for 6 to 7 minutes, until fork-tender. If you prefer, you can also bake them in the oven at 400°F (200°C) for about 1 hour.

3. While the potatoes are still warm, peel them (the skins should easily slide off), then use a potato ricer, masher, or fork to mash them in a large bowl.

4. Add the ricotta, Parmesan, egg yolk, salt, and pepper to the bowl and mix with a fork.

5. Add half the flour to the bowl and lightly stir to incorporate.

6. Pour the mixture onto a floured work surface, then sprinkle the remaining flour on top.

7. Use your hands to gently knead the dough, until the flour is just incorporated. (Be careful not to overwork the dough. It should be sticky and moist and feel like mashed potatoes, but not so sticky that you can't roll it with your hands.) Roll the dough into a ball.

8. Use a bench scraper or large knife to slice the dough into six pieces. We'll be working with one piece at a time. Cover the remaining dough with a bowl or kitchen towel so it doesn't dry out.

9. Sprinkle some flour over the piece of dough and roll it into a rope about ¾ inch (2 cm) in diameter. Cut the rope into ¾-inch (2 cm) pieces. Repeat with the remaining dough.

10. Cook the pieces as is or, for a more traditional shape, roll them on a gnocchi board or on the back of a fork to create ridges. To do this, sprinkle the pieces with flour and place one on your gnocchi board. Use your thumb to gently press the gnocchi into the board and roll down.

11. Bring a pot of salted water to a boil, then add the gnocchi. Cook for 30 seconds to 1 minute, until the gnocchi float to the surface.

3

CHAPTER THREE

Adding Color

When I first started posting videos of my pasta making on social media, I didn't tell anyone I knew. I didn't share the account on my personal pages or ask any friends or family to follow me. I figured if I gave up on my new hobby after a few weeks, I could just delete the account and it would be like the whole thing never happened.

Even though I was having a lot of fun with it, I didn't know how long the account would last. What really pushed me to keep going was the community of pasta lovers on TikTok who followed me and engaged with my content. Still to this day, my TikTok community is one of my biggest sources of inspiration and, more than anything, has helped shape me into the pasta maker I am now. Followers pushed me to be more creative, asking for different colors, shapes, and ingredients. I became inspired by watching chefs, artists, jewelry makers, and fashion designers show off their skills. And some of my most popular ideas have come directly from my followers' comments, from Pride Month pasta to penguin ravioli to holiday-themed meals. I'm extremely grateful to everyone who has interacted with my content and helped me on my pasta-making journey. One of the greatest joys has been seeing people recreate my pasta shapes or come up with their own—I love when people send me pictures of the fresh pasta they've made at home!

The most common questions I get asked on social media are about how I make pasta in different colors. Once people find out I don't use any artificial food coloring, they want to know what ingredients I add to the dough to make it so colorful. How do I make blue pasta? Purple? Pink? This chapter gives you all the information you need to make every color of the rainbow, and then some. The process generally involves pureeing a vegetable like spinach or beets (or adding a powder like turmeric or paprika) and mixing it with eggs and flour to make a dough. For each recipe that uses a vegetable, I've listed a shortcut you can take instead: a powder you can add that will make the process go a little faster.

Beet Pasta Dough (Red)

PREP TIME 1 HR, PLUS 1 HR REST TIME | 4 to 6 SERVINGS

Beets are a humble vegetable. They grow in the dirt and don't look that exciting from the outside, but slice one open and you'll find one of the most magnificent colors that nature has to offer. It's a bold, beautiful deep reddish-purple color that creates some truly stunning pasta. This recipe calls for fresh beets, but I've had success using precooked beets or even canned ones, if you're looking for a quicker option. The beet taste is subtle, and the color may fade slightly while cooking, but you'll still have beautiful pasta that ranges from hot pink to magenta, depending on the beets.

1 medium beet, trimmed

2 large eggs

250 g (1¾ cups) 00 flour

150 g (¾ cup) semola flour

1. Bring a small pot of water to a boil, then add the beet and cook for about 40 minutes, or until fork-tender.

2. Cool the beet under running water, then peel it.

3. Puree the beet and eggs in a blender until you have a smooth magenta mixture.

4. Combine the flours in a pile on a flat work surface or in a large bowl. Make a deep well in the middle.

5. Pour the beet mixture into the well and use a fork to start incorporating the flour.

6. Follow the steps for making Classic Pasta Dough (page 38). Depending on the size of your beet, you may need to adjust the moisture content of the dough. If it's very dry and doesn't come together into a ball, add a spoonful of water. If it's slimy or sticking to your hands, sprinkle on a little extra 00 flour.

NOTE

Even after kneading your dough, it may not feel as smooth and silky as the Classic Pasta Dough (page 38), since it's filled with beet fibers. That's okay!

SHORTCUT

If you want the beautiful beet color but don't have time to boil beets, use beetroot powder. You can find it online, and you just need to whisk or blend together 2 to 3 tablespoons with the eggs when making Classic Pasta Dough (page 38).

BEET PASTA DOUGH WITH PAPRIKA

For a more vibrant red dough, add 1 tablespoon paprika to the beet puree in Step 3. This color is perfect for Santa Hats (page 179).

Roasted Red Pepper Pasta Dough (Orange)

PREP TIME 50 MIN, PLUS 1 HR REST TIME | 4 to 6 SERVINGS

When I was a kid, my father would often roast red peppers on the weekends, and I'd wake up to their aroma filling the house. I still think of him whenever I make them, and though it's easy to buy a jar at the store, it's worth it to roast your own if you have the time. They don't take much effort, last up to a week in the fridge, and are so much more flavorful than the store-bought variety. Either way, they'll give your pasta a beautiful orange color and subtle pepper flavor.

2 medium red bell peppers, halved lengthwise, stemmed, and seeded

2 large eggs

250 g (1¾ cups) 00 flour

150 g (¾ cup) semola flour

1. Preheat the oven to 475°F (245°C). Line a baking sheet with parchment paper or a reusable mat and place the peppers on it, cut side down.

2. Roast for about 25 minutes or until the top layer starts to look black and charred. Be careful not to leave them in too long or they will burn completely.

3. Remove the peppers from the oven and place them in a bowl, then cover the bowl with a kitchen towel.

4. After about 20 minutes, or when the peppers are cool enough to touch, peel off the blackened outer layer. It should slide right off.

5. Puree the peppers and eggs in a blender to form a smooth orange mixture.

6. Combine the flours in a pile on a flat work surface or in a large bowl. Make a deep well in the middle.

7. Pour the pepper mixture into the well and use a fork to start incorporating the flour.

8. Follow the steps for making Classic Pasta Dough (page 38). Depending on the size of your peppers, you may need to adjust the moisture content of your dough. If it's very dry and doesn't come together into a ball, add a spoonful of water. If it's slimy or sticking to your hands, sprinkle on a little extra 00 flour.

NOTE
Even after kneading your dough, it may not feel as smooth and silky as the Classic Pasta Dough (page 38), since it's filled with pepper fibers. That's okay!

SHORTCUT
Paprika is made from dried red peppers, and it's a great ingredient for making orange dough when you're short on time. Add 1 tablespoon to the eggs when making Classic Pasta Dough (page 38).

BURNT ORANGE PASTA DOUGH
To make a burnt orange pasta dough, leave out the bell peppers and instead add 2 tablespoons of paprika to the eggs when making Classic Pasta Dough (page 38).

Turmeric Pasta Dough (Yellow)

PREP TIME 20 MIN, PLUS 1 HR REST TIME | 4 to 6 SERVINGS

Your spice cabinet is the perfect place to look when adding color to your pasta. Spices are quite simple to use in pasta making (there's no need for blanching, roasting, or pureeing like with vegetables), but they can still produce vibrant, beautiful colors. Saffron, curry powder, ginger, and paprika can all be added to pasta dough, although my personal favorite spice to use is turmeric. Egg yolks already give fresh pasta a pale yellow color, but sometimes that's just not enough! Turmeric will give you a bright, deep yellow that is perfect for pasta flowers, suns, rainbows, and more.

4 large eggs

1 tablespoon ground turmeric

250 g (1¾ cups) 00 flour

150 g (¾ cup) semola flour

1. Combine the eggs and turmeric in a medium bowl and mix vigorously until you have a smooth, even color. Alternatively, puree the eggs and turmeric together in a blender.

2. Combine the flours in a pile on a flat work surface or in a large bowl. Make a deep well in the middle.

3. Pour the egg mixture into the middle of the flour, and then follow the recipe for Classic Pasta Dough (page 38).

TIP

Turmeric is notorious for staining clothes and countertops alike. Baking soda is a good ingredient to have on hand if your work surface starts to sprout some deep yellow spots.

Spinach Pasta Dough (Green)

PREP TIME 25 MIN, PLUS 1 HR REST TIME | 4 to 6 SERVINGS

Italians have been adding spinach to their pasta dough for generations, and it's easy to see why. The bright, speckled green dough produces gorgeous-looking pasta, and the spinach gives it a subtle, earthy flavor that perfectly complements a good tomato sauce. One of my favorite pastas to make is a simple spinach noodle—no polka dots or stripes, just a beautiful, bold, green pasta. Once you've learned to make spinach dough, try using other leafy greens—basil, parsley, mint, and kale each produce their own delightful color and flavor.

225 g (8 ounces) spinach

3 large eggs

250 g (1¾ cups) 00 flour

150 g (¾ cup) semola flour

1. Bring a large pot of water to a boil. Fill a large bowl halfway with ice, then add enough cold water until all of the ice is floating.

2. Once the water is boiling, add the spinach and cook for about 30 seconds (see Note 1). Transfer the spinach to the bowl of ice water. Let cool.

3. Drain the water and dry the spinach with a kitchen towel. Try to wring out as much water as possible.

4. Puree the spinach and eggs for 1 to 2 minutes in a blender to form a smooth green mixture.

5. Combine the flours in a pile on a flat work surface or in a large bowl. Make a deep well in the middle.

6. Pour the spinach mixture into the well and use a fork to start incorporating the flour.

7. Follow the steps for making Classic Pasta Dough (page 38). Depending on the amount of water in the spinach, you may need to adjust the moisture content of your dough. If it's very dry and doesn't come together into a ball, add a spoonful of water. If it's slimy or sticking to your hands, sprinkle on a little extra 00 flour.

NOTES

1. Blanching the spinach brings out its green color without cooking the leaves too much.

2. Even after kneading your dough, it may not feel as smooth and silky as the Classic Pasta Dough (page 38), since it's filled with spinach fibers. That's okay!

SHORTCUT

Skip the spinach entirely and add a tablespoon or two of spirulina powder to your eggs before making the Classic Pasta Dough (page 38). I love the deep, hunter green color you get from spirulina, so it's a staple in my pasta making around Christmastime!

Vegan Spinach Pasta Dough (Green)

PREP TIME 25 MIN, PLUS 1 HR REST TIME | 4 to 6 SERVINGS

Just because you're leaving out the eggs doesn't mean you need to leave out the color! In fact, you may find that this pasta is even more vibrant, because there are no yellow yolks to interfere with the other ingredients. Adding spinach also makes the dough a bit sturdier than a typical vegan dough; I've had some great success using this dough for some of the more intricate shapes in this book, like Funghetti (page 114), Barchette (page 99), and Christmas Tree Ravioli (page 169).

225 g (8 ounces) spinach

120 ml (½ cup) water

250 g (1¾ cups) 00 flour

150 g (¾ cup) semola flour

1. Bring a large pot of water to a boil. Fill a large bowl halfway with ice, then add enough cold water until all of the ice is floating.

2. Once the water is boiling, add the spinach and cook for about 30 seconds (see Note 1). Transfer the spinach to the bowl of ice water. Let cool.

3. Drain the water and dry the spinach with a kitchen towel. Try to wring out as much water as possible.

4. Puree the spinach and water in a blender to form a smooth green mixture (see Note 2).

5. Combine the flours in a pile on a flat work surface or in a large bowl. Make a deep well in the middle.

6. Pour the spinach mixture into the well and use a fork to start incorporating the flour.

7. Follow the steps for making Vegan Pasta Dough (page 41). Because the amount of water in your spinach will vary, you may need to adjust the moisture content of your dough. If it's very dry and doesn't come together into a ball, add a spoonful of water. If it's slimy or sticking to your hands, sprinkle on a little extra 00 flour.

SHORTCUT

To make a quick green dough, add a spoonful of spirulina. You can also get a beautiful green color from other powders, such as matcha or wheatgrass powder.

ALL-00 VEGAN SPINACH DOUGH

To make a vegan spinach dough that's easier to roll out by hand, leave out the semola flour and use 400 g (2¾ cups) 00 flour.

NOTES

1. Blanching the spinach brings out its green color without cooking the leaves too much.

2. I know I asked you to wring out as much water from the spinach as possible, only to then add water back in. This is because most blenders will have difficulty pureeing spinach unless there is enough additional liquid.

3. Even after kneading your dough, it may not feel as smooth and silky as a traditional dough, since it's filled with spinach fibers. That's okay!

Vegan Harissa Pasta Dough (Orange)

PREP TIME 20 MIN, PLUS 1 HR REST TIME | 4 to 6 SERVINGS

Harissa is a spicy chili paste that originated in Tunisia and is an important ingredient in Middle Eastern and North African cooking. It can be added to soups or stews, used as a marinade, spread on toast, mixed with hummus—the options for this incredibly versatile spread are pretty much endless. When used in pasta dough, it creates a beautiful orange color similar to the Roasted Red Pepper Pasta Dough on page 53 (which isn't too surprising, since the number one ingredient in harissa is peppers) but speckled with little red dots. Once it's cooked, this pasta will have a subtle, peppery flavor that will give your dish a kick.

100 g (3½ ounces) harissa (see Note)

100 ml (¼ cup plus 3 tablespoons) water

250 g (1¾ cups) 00 flour

150 g (¾ cup) semola flour

1. Mix the harissa and water in a small bowl with a fork until well combined.

2. Combine the flours in a pile on a flat work surface or in a large bowl. Make a deep well in the middle.

3. Pour the harissa mixture into the well and use a fork to start incorporating the flour.

4. Follow the steps for making Vegan Pasta Dough (page 41). Because the amount of water in your harissa will vary, you may need to adjust the moisture content of your dough. If it's very dry and doesn't come together into a ball, add a spoonful of water. If it's slimy or sticking to your hands, sprinkle on a little extra 00 flour.

NOTE

Harissa is available at many grocery stores, but there's no one standard recipe. Different brands will taste somewhat different; some have a smokier flavor, some are spicier, and some are a little sweeter. I recommend looking for ones with peppers as the main ingredient and trying a few different brands to find your favorite.

Blue Pasta Dough

PREP TIME 20 MIN, PLUS 1 HR REST TIME | 4 to 6 SERVINGS

People often ask me how I make blue pasta using natural ingredients. Blue's certainly not the most common color seen in food, and unfortunately blueberries tend to give dough a drab gray color. Allow me to introduce you to two ingredients you might not have heard of before: butterfly pea flower and blue spirulina. Butterfly pea is a beautiful plant, native to Thailand, whose flowers have been brewed as a tea for generations. You can buy the dried flowers in a powdered version online. Blue spirulina is derived from algae and is also sold online in powder form. This recipe leaves out both the egg yolks and the semola flour, as their yellow color will combine with the blue to make green.

6 egg whites

2 teaspoons blue spirulina or 1 tablespoon butterfly pea flower powder, divided (see Note)

400 g (2¾ cups) 00 flour

1. Blend the egg whites and half the spirulina or butterfly pea flower in a blender until smooth. This gives you a close approximation of what your final color will be. Add more spirulina or butterfly pea flower until you are happy with the color.

2. Place the flour in a pile on a flat work surface or in a large bowl. Make a deep well in the middle.

3. Follow the steps for making Classic Pasta Dough (page 38), but keep in mind that the dough will not feel as smooth since it contains no egg yolks.

NOTE

I find that using butterfly pea flower gives the dough more of a matte blue while spirulina leads to a brighter color, but both are lovely.

FOOD FACT

Butterfly pea flower tea changes color when it interacts with an acid. If you brew a cup of this tea and add some lemon juice, the result is a beautiful purple color.

Cabbage Pasta Dough (Purple)

PREP TIME 25 MIN, PLUS 1 HR REST TIME | 4 to 6 SERVINGS

Purple might seem like a tricky color to make using all-natural ingredients, but there are actually a few different ways to get there. The first will bring you back to elementary school art class, where we all learned that mixing red and blue makes purple. You can make a purple dough by adding a spoonful or two of butterfly pea flower or blue spirulina to the beet puree in the Beet Pasta Dough recipe (page 50). Or you can use red cabbage to make a beautiful lavender dough, as shown here. Finally, if you're looking for a bolder, brighter purple, you'll find instructions for using purple sweet potatoes at the bottom of this page.

¼ of a red cabbage (about the size of a baseball), sliced

2 large eggs

250 g (1¾ cups) 00 flour

150 g (¾ cup) semola flour

1. Bring a large pot of water to a boil. Fill a large bowl halfway with ice, then add enough cold water until all the ice is floating.

2. Add the cabbage to the boiling water. Cook for about 30 seconds, then transfer the cabbage to the bowl of ice water (see Note 1). Let cool.

3. Drain the water and dry the cabbage with a kitchen towel.

4. Blend the cabbage and eggs in a blender to form a smooth purple mixture.

5. Combine the flours in a large bowl or on a flat work surface. Make a deep well in the middle.

6. Pour in the cabbage mixture and use a fork to start incorporating the flour.

7. Follow the steps for making Classic Pasta Dough (page 38). Depending on the water content of the cabbage, you may need to adjust the moisture content of your dough. If it's very dry and doesn't come together into a ball, add a spoonful of water. If it's slimy or sticking to your hands, sprinkle on a little extra 00 flour.

NOTES

1. Blanching the cabbage brings out its purple color without cooking it too much.
2. Even after kneading your dough, it may not feel as smooth and silky as the Classic Pasta Dough (page 38), since it's filled with cabbage fibers. That's okay!

PURPLE SWEET POTATO PASTA DOUGH

For a deeper, brighter purple dough, you can use purple sweet potato powder, which is sold online. Mix 6 egg whites with 1 or 2 tablespoons of the powder, then knead together with 400 g (2¾ cups) of 00 flour.

Other Colors

The recipes in this chapter contain only some of the many ingredients you can use to add color to your pasta dough. Peas, saffron, carrots, kale, milk, chestnut flour, and even red wine can all be added to flour and eggs to make bright, vibrant noodles. The process is generally always the same: Turn the ingredient into a puree or a powder, add it to the eggs and flour, mix, and knead it into a dough. Here are a few other colors to try.

White Pasta Dough

If you use all 00 flour to make the Vegan Pasta Dough (page 41), you'll end up with a very usable white dough. You'll face an issue, though, if you're trying to make stripes or another pattern that uses some of the white dough (without eggs) and another color (with eggs). The two doughs will have different textures and pliability, and they won't roll out evenly. To counteract that problem, make a white dough using only egg whites by combining 400 g (2¾ cups) of 00 flour and 6 egg whites. Then follow the recipe for Classic Pasta Dough (page 38).

Pink Pasta Dough

Using a small amount of beetroot powder or pureed beets will give you a light magenta pasta, but if you're going for more of a delicate pink, you can use dragon fruit powder, which is available online. Simply add one or two spoonfuls to the eggs when making Classic Pasta Dough (page 38). One warning: Dragon fruit pasta tends to fade more than other colors when cooked, so roll your dough as thin as possible so it doesn't have to cook very long.

Black Pasta Dough

There are two main ways to get black pasta dough: squid ink (or, more precisely, cuttlefish ink) and activated charcoal powder. They are both available online, and all you need to do is mix a spoonful or two with eggs and then combine with flour when making Classic Pasta Dough (page 38). Both ingredients can be a bit stubborn about incorporating well with the flour, so you may have to knead this dough a bit longer than normal. Some people avoid charcoal powder because it interacts with certain medications, so I recommend doing some research before using it.

Mint Green Pasta Dough

My recipe for Blue Pasta Dough (page 61) leaves out the egg yolks, since their yellow color turns the dough green, but sometimes a light green color is just what you're going for. When making the Classic Pasta Dough (page 38), add 1½ teaspoons of butterfly pea flower powder to the eggs before mixing with the flour. The result is a mint green color that I often use to make Succulent Ravioli (page 161).

Brown Pasta Dough

This dough uses cocoa powder to make a rich brown color, but before you shy away from adding such a sweet ingredient, you should know that chocolate pasta is actually a traditional Italian dish! It's believed to have originated in Umbria and is traditionally served on All Saints' Day, the day after Halloween. Simply add 2 tablespoons of cocoa powder to the Classic Pasta Dough (page 38) when adding the eggs. You may need to add an additional spoonful or two of water to counteract the additional dry ingredient.

4

CHAPTER FOUR

Creating Patterns

Before I started my journey as a pasta maker, I spent ten years working as a lawyer. When I was fresh out of law school, I got a job at a large corporate law firm in New York City. I quickly realized it wasn't for me, so once my student loans were paid off, I started working at a wonderful nonprofit legal services organization. As a housing attorney, I fought every day to keep people in their homes and out of shelters, and to make sure they had safe living conditions. It was rewarding work, and I had amazing coworkers. I thought I'd have this job for many years, if not for the rest of my career.

And yet here I am, no longer a lawyer and doing something I never could have imagined. This transition was an important lesson for me that you never really know where life will take you or how your path will unfold. It taught me that taking risks is okay, and these risks can be made a whole lot less scary if you have a strong support system to catch you if you fall. I'm grateful that my husband and family have been with me for this entire journey, providing their support and love.

I like to think my pasta making embodies a similar spirit, where taking risks is encouraged but, at the end of the day, you'll be loved no matter what. After all, it's only pasta; it's not the end of the world if one of your attempts doesn't work out. I've had more than my fair share of pasta failures, from designs that didn't quite work to ingredients that didn't taste great (I wasn't a big fan of strawberry pasta). This chapter is all about taking your pasta to the next level and taking a few risks to make some beautiful patterns. For all of these patterns, I've suggested colors that work well together, but feel free to experiment with your own. Then, once you've made your pattern, choose one of the shapes from chapters 5 and 6 to make some truly beautiful pasta!

Wide Stripes

PREP TIME 45 MIN | 6 to 8 SERVINGS

Striped pasta is an excellent pattern to start with when you begin your journey as a pasta artist. The process is simple and the results are impressive—I mean, how many times have you seen striped pasta in your life?—and once you've learned the basics, you can really start experimenting. Use two colors or the whole rainbow, make each strip the same width or vary them, or make the perfect holiday-themed pasta. You can do red and green for Christmas, orange and black for Halloween, or even the colors of your favorite sports team. For this recipe, I'm using six colors to make rainbow pasta, but this technique works no matter what colors you choose.

¼ batch Beet Pasta Dough (page 50)

¼ batch Roasted Red Pepper Pasta Dough (page 53)

¼ batch Turmeric Pasta Dough (page 54)

¼ batch Spinach Pasta Dough (page 57)

¼ batch Blue Pasta Dough (page 61)

¼ batch Purple Sweet Potato Pasta Dough (page 62)

Semolina flour, for dusting

1. Roll each color separately through the widest setting of your pasta machine. Laminate each dough by folding it into thirds and running it through the machine again, then repeating this several times (see page 35 for more information). Run each dough through the machine at the widest setting one last time to form a loose rectangle. If you're not using a machine, roll each color into a rectangle about ¼ inch (6 mm) thick. The goal is for each rectangle to be a similar length and width, but it doesn't have to be perfect.

2. Dust a cutting board with flour.

3. Cut each rectangle into long strips about ¾ inch (2 cm) wide.

4. Line up 6 strips, one for each color, next to each other in rainbow order. Press them together so their edges are touching and they stick to each other. Leave the remaining strips covered with a kitchen towel so they don't dry out while you're working (see Tip 1 on page 71).

5. Trim the top and bottom edges of the dough to form a nice clean rectangle.

6. Roll over the dough several times with a rolling pin to flatten it slightly and to make sure the colors are stuck together. Then either continue rolling the dough until it's about 1 millimeter thick or use a pasta machine: Run the pasta through the machine at the widest setting, then keep running it through thinner and thinner settings until you reach the second- or third-thinnest setting.

7. Lay the sheet of pasta on a piece of parchment paper or floured surface and cover with a kitchen towel so it doesn't dry out. Repeat the process with the remaining dough. Then you're ready to cut and fold it into shapes (see chapters 5 and 6).

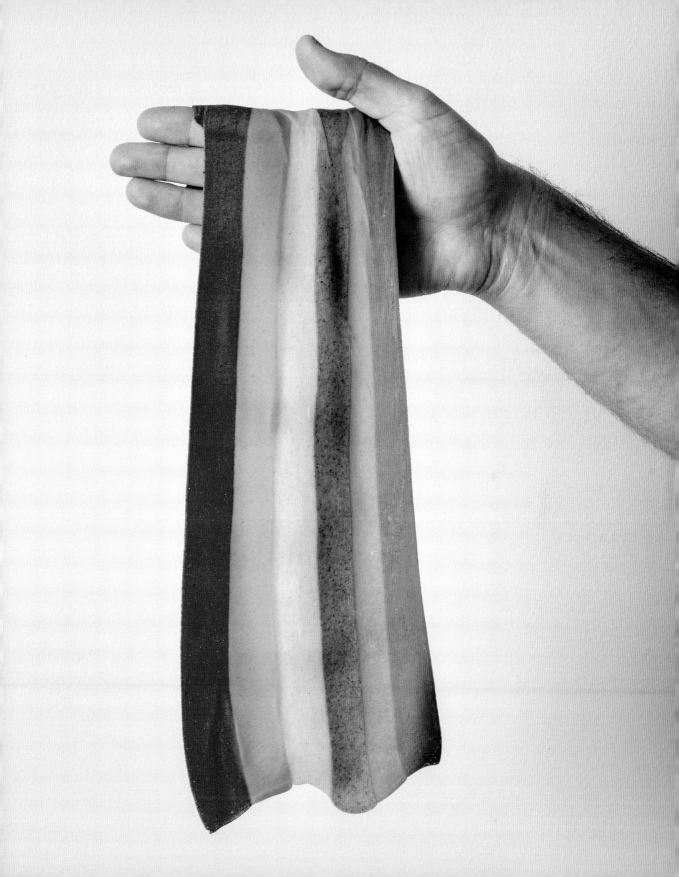

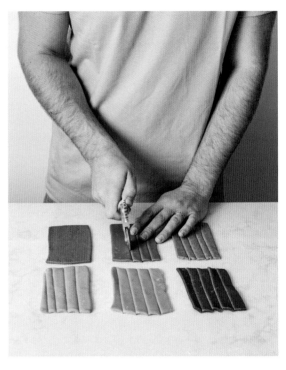

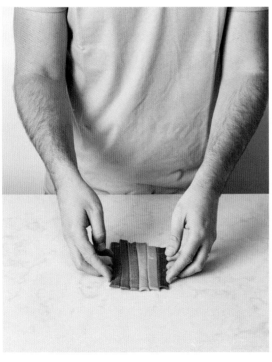

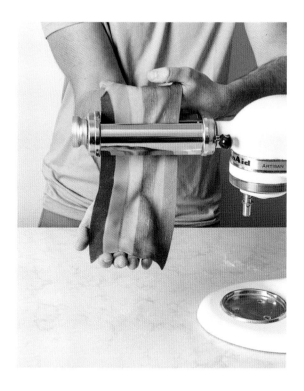
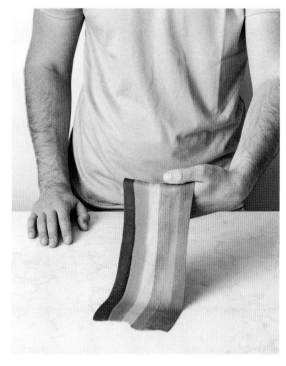

TIPS

1. Depending on how dry your dough is, it may be difficult to get the colors to stick to each other. If they're not sticking, use a paper towel or brush to rub a small amount of water onto the edges of each strip, then gently push them together until they start to stick. You may need to nudge them together and press down on the seams to ensure they are firmly stuck together.

2. When deciding what pattern to make, it's helpful to think about the size of your final shape. If you're making a small shape like Farfalle (page 107), don't make your stripes too wide or only one or two of them will show up on each piece of pasta.

3. When making striped dough, you can vary the width of each color to make different patterns, as long as the stripes are about the same length. You could cut two colors into perfect ½-inch (1 cm) stripes for a nice clean pattern, or do a ½-inch (1 cm) blue stripe followed by a ⅛-inch (3 mm) black stripe followed by a ¼-inch (6 mm) green stripe. If you're using a pasta machine, the total width of your pattern should not be greater than the width of your machine, otherwise it won't fit.

OMBRE PASTA

This pattern is perfect for making ombre pasta, using varying shades of the same color. I usually use blue pasta for this technique, since it's very easy to adjust the amount of butterfly pea flower powder to get different shades. Make ¼ batch of the White Pasta Dough (page 64), ¼ batch of Blue Pasta Dough (page 61) using ¾ teaspoon butterfly pea flower powder, ¼ batch using 1½ teaspoons butterfly pea flower powder, ¼ batch using 1 tablespoon butterfly pea flower powder, and ¼ batch using 1½ tablespoons butterfly pea flower powder. Then follow the Wide Stripes method. I used this technique to make Long Farfalle (page 143).

Thin Stripes

PREP TIME 60 MIN | 4 to 6 SERVINGS

This pasta is made to impress. They're fancy-looking, with thin, delicate lines, and they'll leave your guests wondering how you possibly could have made them. I promise not to reveal our little secret: These are really not that hard to make. It takes some practice, precision, and time, but once you get the hang of it, you can make these over and over again. Their beauty comes down to your knife skills, so use your sharpest knife and cut with confidence. My trick for super straight lines is to pop the dough in the freezer for a few minutes before cutting, which helps prevent the colors from smushing into each other. This recipe uses two main colors and places a thin black line between them to really make the colors pop, but you can use this technique for any striped pattern you want.

½ batch Pink Pasta Dough (page 64)

½ batch Beet Pasta Dough (page 50)

½ batch Black Pasta Dough (page 65)

Semolina flour, for dusting

1. Run the pink and red doughs separately through a pasta machine starting with the widest setting and then working your way down to the third- or fourth-thinnest setting, or to slightly over 1 millimeter if rolling by hand. Run the black dough through a pasta machine to the thinnest setting, or slightly less than 1 millimeter if rolling by hand.

2. Dust a cutting board with flour. Cut each pasta sheet into 5 × 8-inch (13 × 20 cm) rectangles.

3. Place one of the pink rectangles onto your work surface, then place a black rectangle directly on top. Roll the dough lightly with a rolling pin, applying just enough pressure to make sure the layers are stuck together and there are no air bubbles. Then add a red rectangle, roll the dough lightly, and then add another black layer (see Tip on page 74).

4. Continue layering the rectangles, rolling each layer gently to ensure there are no air bubbles, until your stack is 1 to 2 inches (2.5 to 5 cm) high.

5. Position the stack horizontally on your surface. Use a long, sharp knife to slice the stack vertically down the middle to create two identical rectangles that are each about 5 × 4 inches (13 × 10 cm). Place one on top of the other and press down to make sure the two pieces are stuck together and there are no air bubbles.

6. Slice the stack of dough vertically down the middle again to create two 5 × 2-inch (13 × 10 cm) rectangles. Place one on top of the other. Press down on all sides of the stack to make sure the layers are stuck together and there are no large air bubbles.

7. Place the pasta stack in the freezer for about 15 minutes, until firm but not frozen solid. Remove the pasta from the freezer and place it vertically on a cutting board.

8. In one firm motion, cut the stack into long slices as thin as you reasonably can, ideally less than ¼ inch (6 mm). The first and last slices might be a little messy, but the rest should lie flat.

9. Trim the edges of each slice to form nice, tidy rectangles. Cover the rectangles with a kitchen towel so they don't dry out as you're working.

10. Run each slice through your pasta machine until you reach the second- or third-thinnest setting, or use a rolling pin to roll out the pasta in the direction of the lines until it's about 1 millimeter thick.

11. Lay the sheet of pasta on a piece of parchment paper or floured surface and cover with a kitchen towel so it doesn't dry out. Repeat the process with the remaining dough. Then you're ready to cut and fold it into shapes (see chapters 5 and 6).

TIP

If the dough feels dry and the layers are not sticking together, brush each layer with a damp paper towel before placing them on top of each other, so they stick.

Polka Dots

PREP TIME 60 MIN | 4 to 6 SERVINGS

Most people probably don't think of pasta as an artistic medium, and I can't say I really blame them. After all, I've never seen a plate of pasta in a museum or art history textbook. But with this method, you can make some truly museum-worthy pasta, and the only limit is your imagination. This recipe makes polka dot pasta, but the same technique can be used to make plaids, florals, or even a pasta portrait or lasagna Mona Lisa if you're feeling brave! (See the variations on page 78 for more ideas.) I've chosen red and yellow as the color palette for this pasta, but feel free to swap in any other colors you'd like.

1 batch Beet Pasta
Dough (page 50)

½ batch Turmeric
Pasta Dough
(page 54)

Semolina flour, for
dusting

TIPS

1. Be careful—your design may get distorted as you run it through the pasta machine. To counteract this, run the pasta sheet through the machine, then run it again in the opposite direction. This should gently nudge the design back into place.

2. If you're worried about your pasta falling apart, go over the sheet with a rolling pin once or twice to make sure everything is secure, then wait about 10 minutes before cooking to let the shapes dry into place.

1. Cut the beet dough into quarters and work with one piece at a time, leaving the rest covered so it doesn't dry out. Roll the dough to the second-thinnest or thinnest setting on your pasta machine, or to about 1 millimeter if rolling by hand.

2. Dust your work surface with flour and place the pasta sheet down.

3. Cut the turmeric dough into quarters and work with one piece at a time, leaving the rest covered. Roll the dough to the thinnest setting on your pasta machine, or as thin as you can if rolling by hand.

4. Lightly dust a cutting board with flour and place the turmeric pasta sheet down. Using a circular plunger cutter or a knife, cut out a sheet of ½-inch (1 cm) circles.

5. Using a brush or paper towel, lightly brush the sheet of red dough with a thin layer of water.

6. Place your yellow circles carefully on the red dough. Once they stick, they can be hard to move, so be thoughtful here!

7. Gently press the yellow pieces into the red dough to make sure they stick. Working quickly but carefully, fill the entire sheet with polka dots.

8. If you're making a pasta shape with a lot of bends or curves, roll the dough into one smooth sheet so the circles don't pop off. Roll the dough with a rolling pin until smooth or run it through your pasta machine (see Tip 1).

9. If you're making a flat shape like ravioli, don't worry about rolling your pasta in one smooth sheet. As long as you've pressed the top pieces into the base dough, they won't fall off during the cooking process (see Tip 2).

10. Lay the sheet of pasta on a piece of parchment paper or floured surface and cover with a kitchen towel so it doesn't dry out. Repeat the process with the remaining dough. Then you're ready to cut and fold it into shapes (see chapters 5 and 6).

Reverse Polka Dots

After you cut out a bunch of polka dots, this is an efficient way to use the remaining dough! Gently punch out each polka dot from a sheet of pasta, being careful not to rip any of the remaining dough. After you've removed all the polka dots, you should be left with a sheet of dough that looks like a colorful piece of Swiss cheese. Lay out a sheet of base dough in a different color, then carefully pick up the Swiss cheese dough and place it directly on top. Run over it with a rolling pin a few times or run it through your pasta machine once or twice to make sure it sticks.

Abstract Lines

This is a great design if you have pieces of colored dough left over from another shape. Roll each color to the thinnest setting on your pasta machine, or as thin as you can if rolling by hand, and then cut it into spaghetti using a pasta machine or a knife. Roll out a sheet of Classic Pasta Dough (page 38) and spread the spaghetti on top. Roll over the spaghetti with a rolling pin to create an abstract pattern.

Plaid

Make 1 batch of Classic Pasta Dough (page 38) and ¼ batch of any colored dough. Using the spaghetti attachment on your pasta machine or a knife, cut the colored dough into thin strips. Dust a surface with flour, then lay a sheet of classic dough horizontally onto the surface. Starting with the bottom left corner, place 3 pieces of spaghetti diagonally across the pasta, ¼ inch (6 mm) apart. Leave a gap of about 1½ inches (4 cm) and then place 3 more pieces of spaghetti diagonally across the pasta sheet, ¼ inch (6 mm) apart. Continue this pattern all the way down the pasta sheet. Then, starting with the top left corner, place 3 pieces of spaghetti diagonally across the pasta in the opposite direction so they criss-cross with the original stripes. Leaving gaps of about 1½ inches (4 cm), do this all the way down the dough to form a diagonal plaid pattern. The dough will be raised higher where the lines intersect, making it more likely that the pattern will become distorted when you run it through your pasta machine. To counteract this, press those areas down with your finger to create an even layer.

Cookie-Cutter Patterns

Using small cookie cutters or plunger cutters, cut out several dozen stars, hearts, or other small shapes. Carefully place them onto your base dough, pressing them down slightly to make sure they stick. Get creative! I love using different-sized heart cookie cutters and different colored doughs to make a pattern, but the options are limitless.

Spirals

PREP TIME 60 MIN | 4 to 6 SERVINGS

You might be familiar with this technique if you've ever worked with polymer clay to make jewelry or, perhaps, made one of those Swiss roll cakes that are rolled up like a log. It starts off a bit like the method for making Thin Stripes (page 72), but unlike the other patterns in this chapter, it doesn't produce one big sheet of pasta. Instead, it yields a whole bunch of flat spiral circles that you can turn into individual shapes (my favorites are Farfalle, page 107, and Caramelle, page 134) or stick on a sheet of base dough to make a larger design.

½ batch Classic Pasta Dough (page 38)

½ batch Beet Pasta Dough (page 50)

Semolina flour, for dusting

1. Divide each dough into quarters. Work with one quarter at a time and leave the rest covered. Roll each dough to the second- or third-thinnest setting on your pasta machine, or about 1 millimeter if rolling by hand.

2. Dust a cutting board with flour. Cut each sheet of pasta into a 5 × 12-inch (13 × 30 cm) rectangle.

3. Lay the classic dough rectangle on the cutting board, then place a red rectangle directly on top. Roll the dough lightly with a rolling pin, applying just enough pressure to make sure the layers are stuck together and there are no air bubbles.

4. Trim all the edges to form a neat rectangle.

5. Beginning with one of the short edges of the rectangle, roll the dough into a log as tightly as you can, but being careful not to smush the dough as you roll.

6. Roll the log between your hands or on your work surface to make sure all the layers are tightly stuck together.

7. Put the log in the freezer for about 15 minutes, until firm but not frozen solid.

8. Remove the log from the freezer and slice it into circles as thinly and evenly as possible.

9. To prevent the spirals from becoming distorted, roll them with a rolling pin rather than a pasta machine. Roll each circle out to about 1 millimeter thick.

10. Lay the circles on a piece of parchment paper or floured surface and cover with a kitchen towel so they don't dry out. Repeat the process with the remaining dough. Then you're ready to cut and fold it into shapes (see chapters 5 and 6).

Tie-Dye

PREP TIME 2O MIN | 4 SERVINGS

Certain pasta shapes create a lot of dough scraps, but please don't throw them out! Italians call these irregularly shaped pieces *maltagliati*, and they can be cooked and used just like any other type of pasta. They're also perfect for making tie-dye pasta, as long as you choose your colors carefully. The colors will start to merge in this process, so avoid contrasting colors that will turn your pasta into a brown mush (unless that's what you're going for, of course!). You can make some beautiful tie-dye pasta with different shades of blue, for example, or try for some red, orange, and yellow sunset vibes. Or just mash all the colors you have together—even if it doesn't look great, it will still taste good!

¼ batch Beet Pasta Dough (page 50)

¼ batch Roasted Red Pepper Pasta Dough (page 53)

¼ batch Turmeric Pasta Dough (page 54)

1. Combine the doughs into a large ball and knead for about 30 seconds, until the colors have started to mix together but are still distinct (see Tip 1).

2. Use your hand or a rolling pin to flatten the dough to about ½ inch (1 cm) thick. Run the dough through the widest setting of your pasta machine (see Tip 2) or keep rolling it out by hand to 1 millimeter thick.

3. Trim the edges of the dough to form a rectangle and continue running it through the machine at thinner and thinner settings until the second- or third-thinnest setting, or about 1 millimeter if rolling by hand.

4. Lay the sheet of pasta on a piece of parchment paper or floured surface and cover with a kitchen towel so it doesn't dry out. Repeat the process with the remaining dough. Then you're ready to cut and fold it into shapes (see chapters 5 and 6).

TIPS

1. If you're using scraps of dough to make this tie-dye pasta, collect all of the scraps and roll them into a ball of dough. You may have to knead the dough for a minute or two so all the scraps come together, but be careful not to work the dough too much, to prevent the colors from merging.

2. If you're using scraps, there's a good chance your pasta won't roll through the machine smoothly and will instead come out ripped and shredded with lots of holes in it. Don't fret! This happens if the colors haven't come together yet and is especially likely if some pieces are drier than others. Fold the dough in half or stack the pieces on top of each other and run them through the machine again. You may have to do this several times until the dough has come together.

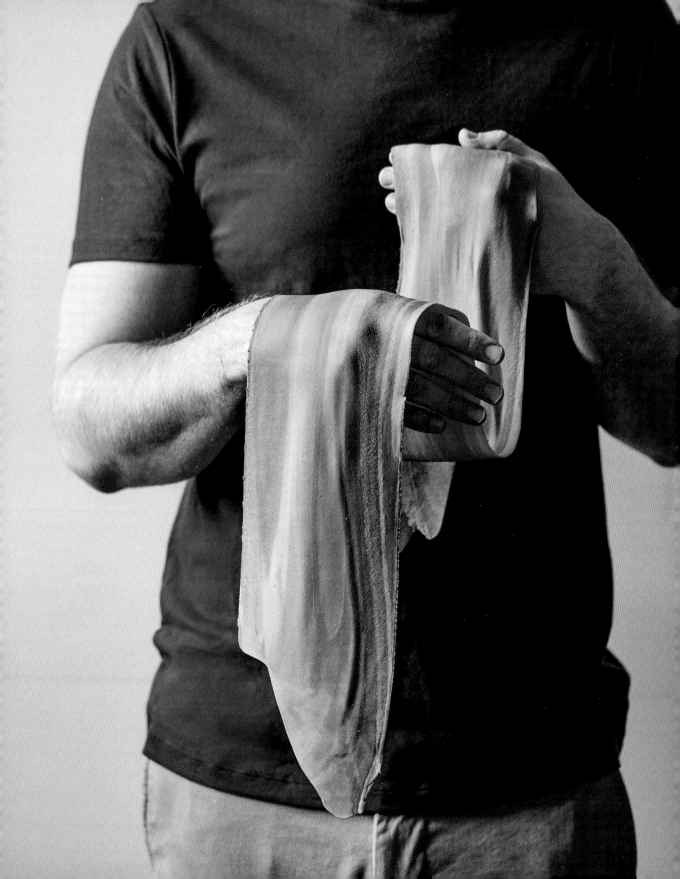

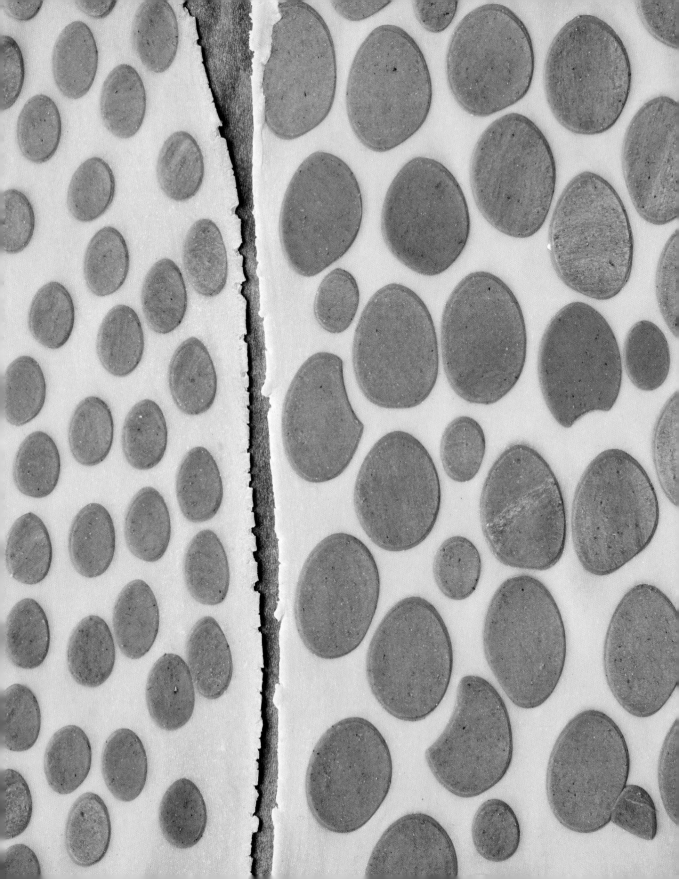

Giraffe Print

PREP TIME 60 MIN | 4 to 6 SERVINGS

A bowl of pasta doesn't remind most people of the animal kingdom, but we're here to change that! With just a few different colors and a sharp knife, you can recreate the jungle on your plate without having to leave your kitchen. The animal prints in this chapter draw heavily from the method described in the recipe for Polka Dots (page 77), so give that a try before you dive into these specific patterns.

1 batch Classic Pasta Dough (page 38)

½ batch Burnt Orange Pasta Dough (page 53)

Semolina flour, for dusting

1. Cut the classic pasta dough into quarters and work with one piece at a time, leaving the rest covered so it doesn't dry out. Roll the dough to the second- or third-thinnest setting on your pasta machine, or about 1 millimeter thick if rolling by hand.

2. Dust your work surface with flour, then lay the pasta sheet on top.

3. Cut the orange dough into quarters and work with one piece at a time, leaving the rest covered so it doesn't dry out. Roll out the dough to the thinnest setting on your pasta machine, or as thin as you can roll it by hand, and lay it down on the floured surface.

4. If you look at a picture of a real giraffe, you'll see they have boxy, irregular markings. You can recreate this look by cutting out small shapes from the orange dough using a sharp paring knife or X-Acto knife. Or, for a faster way, use a circular plunger cutter to cut ¼- to ½-inch (6 mm to 1 cm) diameter circles out of the orange dough.

5. Brush the sheet of base dough with a very small amount of water until it feels sticky. Place the orange circles on the base dough and press down so they stick. Place the circles very close together; they will spread out when we roll the dough again. Fill the entire base sheet with circles.

6. Roll the dough several times with a rolling pin to flatten it and make sure the orange shapes stay in place. If your spots are looking a little too perfect, run the dough through a pasta machine several times in different directions to stretch out the circles. You can also roll over the dough in different directions with a rolling pin.

7. Lay the sheet of pasta on a piece of parchment paper or floured surface and cover with a kitchen towel so it doesn't dry out. Repeat the process with the remaining dough. Then you're ready to cut and fold it into shapes (see chapters 5 and 6).

Leopard Print

PREP TIME 60 MIN | 4 to 6 SERVINGS

We've all seen leopard print on clothing before, so why not pasta? This design uses three colors—classic dough, burnt orange, and black—although you're free to experiment with your own. (Hot pink and purple leopard print ravioli, anyone?) You'll need to do some freehand cutting for this, so I recommend using an X-Acto knife or small paring knife. If you happen to wear a lot of leopard print clothing, head to your closet to get an idea of what we're trying to create, and then get started!

1 batch Classic Pasta Dough (page 38)

½ batch Burnt Orange Pasta Dough (page 53)

½ batch Black Pasta Dough (page 65)

Semolina flour, for dusting

1. Cut the classic pasta dough into quarters and work with one piece at a time, leaving the rest covered so it doesn't dry out. Roll the dough to the second- or third-thinnest setting on your pasta machine, or about 1 millimeter thick if rolling by hand.

2. Dust a work surface with flour, then lay the base dough on top.

3. Cut the orange and black doughs into quarters and work with one piece at a time, leaving the rest covered so it doesn't dry out. Roll out the dough to the thinnest setting on your pasta machine, or as thin as you can roll it by hand, and lay it down on the floured surface.

4. Use a circular plunger cutter or a sharp knife to cut ¼- to ½-inch (6 mm to 1 cm) diameter circles out of the orange dough.

5. Using a small knife, cut horseshoe shapes ¾ inch (2 cm) wide out of the black dough to fit around the orange dots. If you look at photos of leopards, you'll notice that the black fur surrounds the dark orange spots but doesn't make a complete circle. Try to cut out a similar shape.

6. Brush the base dough with a very small amount of water until it feels sticky. Place the orange circles on the base dough and press down so they stay in place, then wrap a black horseshoe around each orange circle. Place the spots very close together; they will spread out when you roll the dough again. Fill the entire sheet with spots.

7. Roll out the dough several times with a rolling pin to flatten it and make sure the spots stay in place. You can also run the dough through a pasta machine several times so the spots stretch out and appear more irregular.

8. Lay the sheet of pasta on a piece of parchment paper or floured surface and cover with a kitchen towel so it doesn't dry out. Repeat the process with the remaining dough. Then you're ready to cut and fold it into shapes (see chapters 5 and 6).

Tiger Print and Zebra Print

PREP TIME 45 MIN | 4 to 6 SERVINGS

Tiger and zebra stripes are rough and uneven, sometimes trailing off and sometimes converging. The stripes in this design are made entirely freehand, so you can make them as large or as small as you'd like. It helps to think about the pasta shape you're planning for this design—if it's something small, like Tortellini (page 125), you'll need to make your stripes pretty narrow; otherwise, you'll end up with a piece of pasta with a large black streak across it. If you're making lasagna or even Ravioli (page 122), large stripes will work better. Either way, the process is the same.

1 batch Roasted Red Pepper Pasta Dough (page 53, for Tiger Print) or White Pasta Dough (page 64, for Zebra Print)

1 batch Black Pasta Dough (page 65)

Semolina flour, for dusting

1. Divide the base dough (orange for tiger print or white for zebra print) into quarters. Working with a quarter at a time and leaving the rest covered, roll out the dough to the second- or third-thinnest setting on your pasta machine, or about 1 millimeter if rolling it out by hand.

2. Dust your work surface with flour, then lay the base dough on top.

3. Divide the black dough into quarters. Working with a quarter at a time and leaving the rest covered, roll out the dough to the thinnest setting on your pasta machine, or as thin as you can if rolling by hand. Lay the sheet down on the floured surface.

4. Using an X-Acto knife or paring knife, cut irregular, wavy stripes out of the black dough to mimic the fur of a tiger or zebra.

5. Brush the sheet of base dough with a very small amount of water until it feels sticky.

6. Lay the stripes on the base dough to create your pattern. Press down slightly so they stay in place.

7. Roll out the dough several times with a rolling pin to flatten it and prevent the stripes from falling off, or run the dough through a pasta machine.

8. Lay the sheet of pasta on a piece of parchment paper or floured surface and cover with a kitchen towel so it doesn't dry out. Repeat the process with the remaining dough. Then you're ready to cut and fold it into shapes (see chapters 5 and 6).

Flower- and Herb-Laminated Dough

PREP TIME 35 MIN | 4 to 6 SERVINGS

This is one of my favorite pasta-making techniques, and the results are simply gorgeous. The faded outline of the leaves, the subtle colors popping through—it all comes together to remind me of a Monet painting with its romantic, yet blurry foliage. On page 35, we talked about laminating the dough, the process of folding it onto itself to help the gluten structures form, but this type of laminating is completely different. It refers to the method of sandwiching fresh herbs and flowers between two thin layers of pasta dough to make beautiful, delicate patterns. You can use any herbs or edible flowers for this, but I recommend ones with soft, small leaves or petals, such as oregano, thyme, parsley, chives, or pansies.

1 batch Classic Pasta Dough (page 38)

2 cups (75 g) herbs or flowers

Semolina flour, for dusting

1. Divide the dough into quarters. Working with one quarter at a time and leaving the rest covered, roll out the dough to the thinnest setting on your pasta machine, or as thin as you can roll it by hand. You want the dough to be almost translucent if you hold it up to the light, so the herbs will shine through.

2. Place your pasta sheet on a floured surface or parchment paper. Use a brush or a paper towel to lightly brush water over the top to moisten slightly.

3. Arrange your herbs or flowers on the pasta in whatever pattern you like, pressing them in slightly so they stick. They will stretch out when you roll the dough, so place them close together.

4. Roll out another sheet of pasta dough as thin as you can. Place that carefully on top of the herbs, doing your best to avoid any large air bubbles.

5. Run the pasta through the machine two to three times or roll it with a rolling pin to seal the herbs inside.

6. Lay the sheet of pasta on a piece of parchment paper or floured surface and cover with a kitchen towel so it doesn't dry out. Repeat the process with the remaining dough. Then you're ready to cut and fold it into shapes (see chapters 5 and 6).

5

CHAPTER FIVE

Traditional Shapes

All pasta is made from just a few simple ingredients, yet one ball of dough can lead to dozens of different shapes. Hundreds, really, if the ball of dough is large enough. Pasta takes up a large amount of space at the grocery store in part because it's extremely popular, but also because there are so many varieties. At almost any supermarket you can find long thin strands of angel hair, or spiral-shaped rotini, or short little tubes like ziti. Even if you narrow down the type of pasta you want, there might be a handful of options. You can choose tubes with flat ends and no ridges (ziti), tubes with angular ends and ridges (penne), tubes with angular ends but no ridges (mostaccioli), or wide tubes with flat ends and ridges (rigatoni). And even then, you can choose between rigatoni and mezze rigatoni, depending on how long you want your tube!

It all can seem a bit unusual or even unnecessary, as if Italians have an overabundance of creativity or an excessive flair for the dramatic. But if you dive deeper into the world of pasta, you'll find a fascinating history. Over time, pasta shapes have been developed regionally and locally, and people in one town might have eaten a shape that you couldn't find anywhere else in Italy. The shapes were also often designed to work perfectly with the cuisine of a particular region. A hefty pasta like rigatoni can withstand a hearty, meaty sauce, while a shape like angel hair might work better for a thin cream sauce.

When you make the recipes in this chapter, you'll be joining the ranks of the many generations of pasta makers who've come before us. Some of these shapes will likely be familiar to you, like the bow-tie shape Farfalle (page 107), while others, like the triangular Fusi Istriani (page 111), might be new. For each recipe, I've included a color or pattern that I think works well for that particular shape, but I encourage you to mix and match and try different colors with different shapes and different sauces. I've thus far resisted the urge to use the word *pastabilities* in this book, but I'll employ it here: The pastabilities are truly endless, and I'm sure you will think of pasta combinations that I haven't tried!

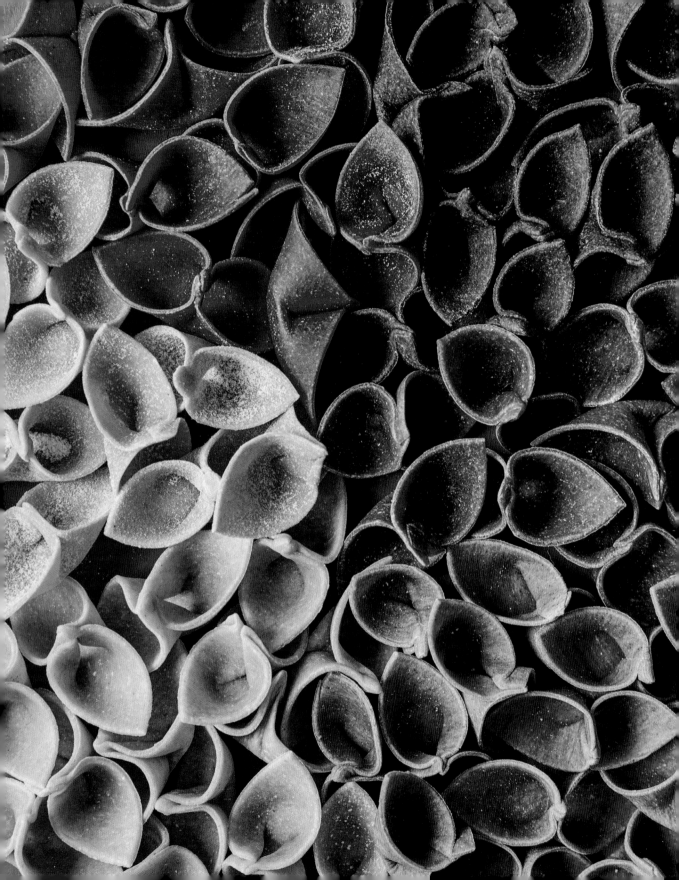

Barchette

PREP TIME 45 MIN | COOK TIME 5 MIN | 4 to 6 SERVINGS

I'm not sure who first developed this shape, but it's been floating (pun intended) around the internet for a while, and I absolutely love it. The name means "little boats," and indeed they look like tiny pasta rowboats gliding across the plate. The two halves are perfect for filling up with sauce or broth (which I suppose is the exact opposite of the way real boats work), and they are one satisfying bite of food. They're small, so they don't show patterns as well as other shapes, but I love to make a bunch of these in different colors and watch them all float in a sea of tomato soup.

1 batch pasta dough,
   any color (see
   chapters 2 and 3)

Semolina flour, for
   dusting

1. Cut the dough into quarters and work with one piece at a time, leaving the rest covered so it doesn't dry out. Roll the dough to the second- or third-thinnest setting on your pasta machine, or about 1 millimeter thick if rolling by hand.

2. Lightly dust a cutting board with flour. Use a sharp knife or pastry roller to cut the dough into 1¼-inch (3 cm) squares.

3. Cover the squares with a bowl or kitchen towel so they don't dry out, and work with one piece at a time.

4. Pick up two opposite corners of the square and bring them toward each other, as if you are folding the square in half, but leave the bottom rounded instead of making a crease. Pinch the two tips of the square together with your thumb and index finger.

5. Rotate your two fingers 90 degrees, so they're now inside the little roll you've made on opposite sides of the pinched top.

6. Squeeze your fingers together to form two rounded bowls and flatten the dividing line of dough between them. Give the center line a good pinch so it stays in place.

7. Rest the pasta on a floured surface or piece of parchment paper. Continue with the rest of the dough.

8. Cook the pasta in salted, boiling water until tender, 2 to 5 minutes.

PASTA FACT

This shape is reminiscent of *lumache*, meaning "snails," which I've seen sold in the United States as *pipette*. They look a bit like fat elbow macaroni with large openings on either end, though one of the ends is pinched closed. This is a great shape for making macaroni and cheese, as they fill up with sauce, making each bite a thing of gooey, cheesy beauty.

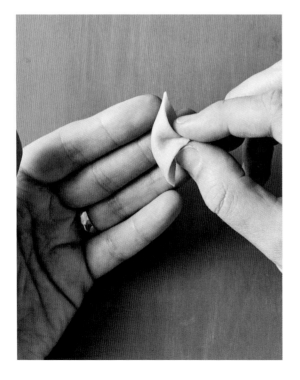

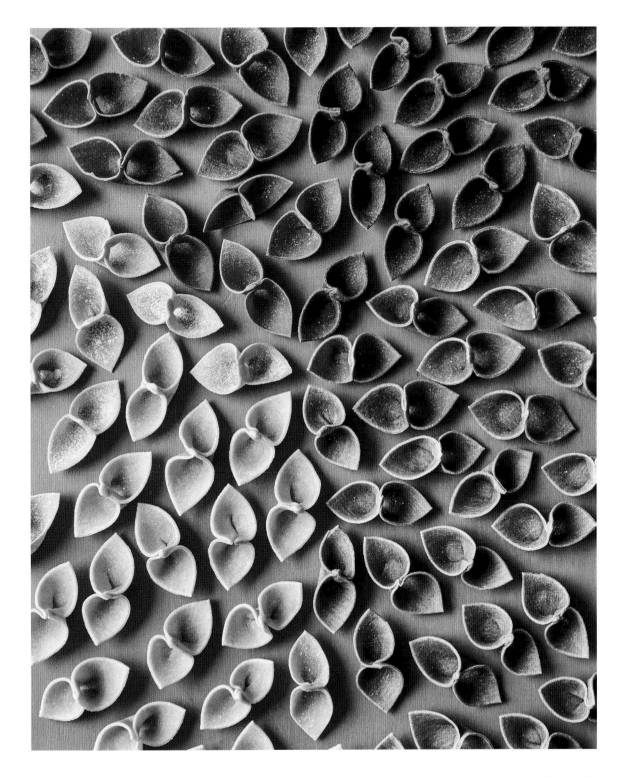

Tagliatelle

PREP TIME 45 MIN | COOK TIME 5 MIN | 4 to 6 SERVINGS

Tagliatelle, fettuccine, linguine—if you're not a pasta aficionado, you could be forgiven for thinking they're the same type of noodle. They are all long strips of pasta that resemble flat spaghetti, but the difference is in their width. A perfect fettuccine is slightly wider than tagliatelle, and linguine is the skinniest of the bunch. I'm not suggesting you break out your ruler, though; I'm a firm believer that pasta doesn't have to be perfect! If you have a pasta machine, it likely has a fettuccine cutter, so you can make it quickly and easily. Tagliatelle is traditionally made by hand, though, so this is the perfect recipe for a quick, delicious pasta that doesn't require any special equipment.

1 batch All-00 Classic Pasta Dough (page 38)

Semolina flour, for dusting

1. Lightly dust your work surface with flour. Divide the dough into quarters, then work with about a quarter at a time and leave the rest covered so it doesn't dry out.

2. Use a rolling pin to roll the dough into a loose rectangular shape about 12 inches (30 cm) long. Roll the dough to about 1 millimeter thick (see Note).

3. Dust both sides of your rectangle with flour. You're going to be folding the dough onto itself, so it's important that the dough is not sticky.

4. Position the dough horizontally on your surface. Fold the dough in half lengthwise, then unfold it to create a crease in the middle.

5. Take each end of the dough and fold it toward the center so the edges of the dough line up with the center crease. Unfold the dough; you should now have four lines in your pasta, separating it into quarters.

6. Take the right end of the pasta and fold it toward the closest line so the edge of the dough lines up with the crease. Fold it over the crease and then fold it one more time over itself so you reach the middle line. Repeat this step with the other side so they both meet in the middle.

7. Using a large knife, slice the dough into strips. A traditional tagliatelle is about ¼ inch (6 mm) wide, but you can make them any width you'd like.

8. Unroll the strips: You've made tagliatelle! If you want to be fancy, you can slip the knife underneath the middle line of the dough and lift it up. The pasta should unfurl quickly!

9. Sprinkle a generous amount of flour over your tagliatelle so they don't stick to each other.

10. Repeat with the remaining dough.

11. Cook the pasta in salted, boiling water until tender, 2 to 5 minutes.

NOTE

You can cut off the edges to make a perfect rectangle if you're a stickler, but there's nothing wrong with leaving it a bit messy. It just means you'll end up with a few wonky noodles.

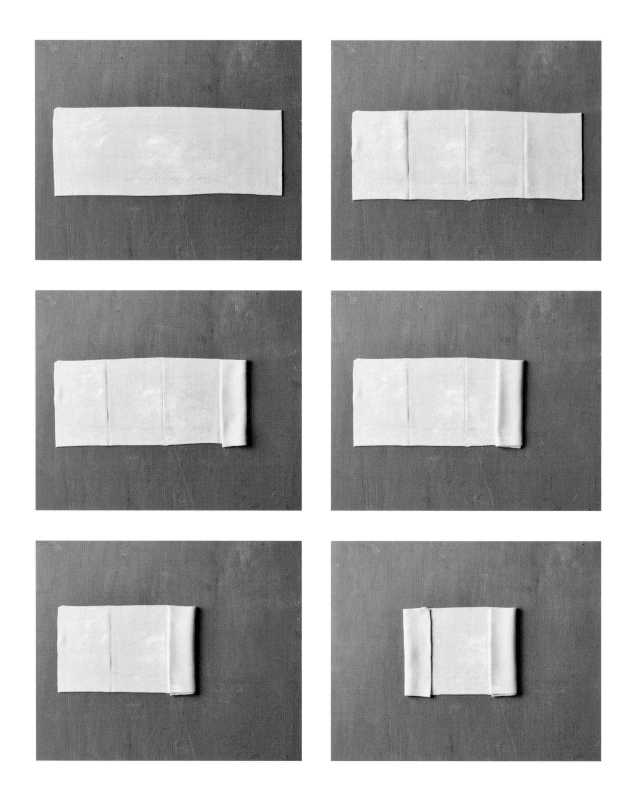

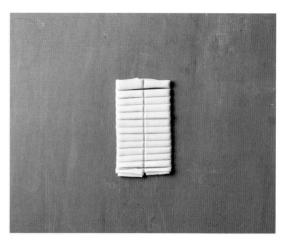

Bologna's Chamber of Commerce houses a golden replica of the perfect tagliatelle, which should measure exactly 8 millimeters wide when cooked. To get this dimension, you'd have to cut your uncooked tagliatelle 6½ to 7 millimeters wide.

Farfalle

PREP TIME 35 MIN | COOK TIME 5 MIN | 4 to 6 SERVINGS

I have two brothers, and when we were kids, we produced our fair share of kindergarten art projects. Somewhere in a box in my parents' attic, there are a few pieces of construction paper with decades-old bow-tie pasta glued to them. Or, more likely, there are the crushed remains of pasta littering the bottom of the box, with perhaps a hole chewed into it by some mice. Bow-tie pasta is a great shape to make by hand because it's fun, quick, and easy. The name in Italian, *farfalle*, actually means "butterflies," and while it may take a few tries to get the folding technique just right, once you have it down, you can make a batch of these in no time. For farfalle, I like to use the wide stripe technique on page 68, though any color or pattern will do.

1 batch Wide Stripes (page 68; see Tip 1 below)

Semolina flour, for dusting

1. Lightly dust a cutting board with flour and place one sheet of pasta down. Leave the others covered with a kitchen towel so they don't dry out while you're working. Use a sharp knife or a pastry roller (see Tip 2) to cut the dough into 2 × 1½-inch (5 × 4 cm) rectangles.

2. Cover the rectangles with a bowl or kitchen towel so they don't dry out, and work with one piece at a time.

3. Hold the rectangle vertically with both hands, as if you're very loosely holding your phone to text someone. Use your thumbs to hold the center of the pasta in place while you pinch the two sides together in the middle, creating two ridges; think of it as a valley between two mountains. Press the two ridges together until they stick (see Tips 3 and 4).

4. Rest the pasta on a floured surface or piece of parchment paper. Continue with the rest of the dough.

5. Cook the pasta in salted, boiling water until tender, 2 to 5 minutes.

PASTA FACT

Although we know this shape as *farfalle* ("butterflies"), it's called *stricchetti*, derived from the word meaning "pinch," in the Emilia-Romagna region of Italy.

TIPS

1. To fit all six colors of the rainbow on this pasta, I made each stripe about ¼ inch (6 mm) wide when following the recipe for Wide Stripes on page 68.

2. I like to use a fluted pastry wheel to cut the short end of the pasta and a regular pastry wheel to cut the long end, but if you don't have those, a regular knife is fine.

3. If your pasta has started to dry out, you may have trouble getting the ridges to stick together. To fix this, use your finger to brush a tiny bit of water between the ridges to act as a glue.

4. If you're having trouble getting the folds just right, place a thin skewer vertically down the middle of your rectangle. That will keep the center in place while you squeeze the two sides together. When you pull the skewer out, the folds should stay in place.

Garganelli

PREP TIME 45 MIN | COOK TIME 5 MIN | 4 to 6 SERVINGS

This is often the first shape that newbie pasta makers tackle when they're ready for something a bit more challenging than Tagliatelle (page 102) or Farfalle (page 107), and it's easy to see why. This is basically the handmade version of penne, that classic shape we all know and love. Legend has it that the shape was born when a hapless Italian housewife was halfway through making Tortellini (page 125), only to discover that her cat had eaten all the filling. With the pasta already cut into squares, she quickly pivoted and rolled each piece onto a stick to create what we now call garganelli. They are traditionally rolled on a pasta comb to create their characteristic ridges, but a gnocchi board, sushi mat, or even an actual comb work as well. As for the stick, most pasta combs come with a small dowel that's the perfect size, but a clean pencil works just fine! It can be difficult to see more intricate patterns on this shape, so I love to use the tie-dye technique on page 84, but feel free to use a solid color or another pattern if you'd like.

1 batch Tie-Dye
  (page 84)

Semolina flour, for
  dusting

1. Lightly dust a cutting board with flour and place one sheet of pasta down. Leave the others covered with a kitchen towel so they don't dry out while you're working. Use a sharp knife or a pastry roller to cut the dough into 1½-inch (4 cm) squares.

2. Cover the squares with a bowl or kitchen towel so they don't dry out, and work with one piece at a time.

3. Dust your dowel (or pencil) and pasta comb with flour.

4. Place a square of pasta diagonally on the pasta comb, so one of the corners is facing you. Lightly dust the pasta with flour, then place the dowel horizontally across the corner closest to you.

5. Hold the closest tip of the pasta in place on the dowel, then roll the dowel away from you so the pasta wraps around it. Firmly press the dowel into the comb as you roll to form ridges on the pasta.

6. Keep rolling the dowel until the pasta forms a complete cylinder. Press firmly as you finish rolling to seal the pasta so it doesn't unroll.

7. Slide the pasta off the dowel and rest it on a floured surface or piece of parchment paper. Continue with the rest of the dough.

8. Cook the pasta in salted, boiling water until tender, 2 to 5 minutes.

PASTA FACT

The name *garganelli* comes from the word *garganel*, which means "chicken's gullet" in a local dialect of the Emilia-Romagna region. They supposedly look like a gullet, another word for esophagus, but I have not verified this myself.

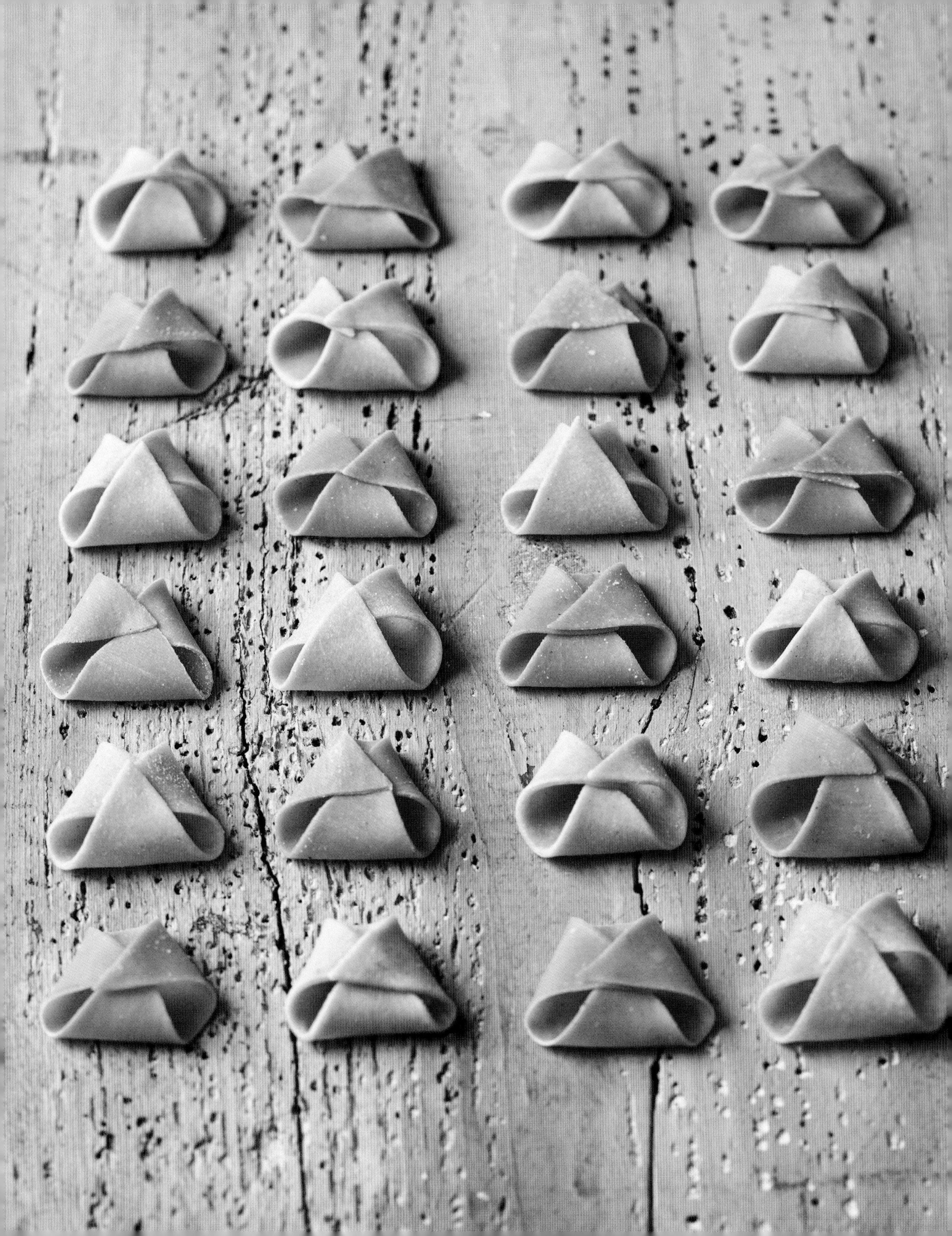

Fusi Istriani

PREP TIME 45 MIN | COOK TIME 5 MIN | 4 to 6 SERVINGS

This beautiful little shape hails from Istria, the peninsula east of Venice that is now shared by Italy, Slovenia, and Croatia. It looks a bit like a triangle that's bubbled up in the sun, and it's made with just a few strategic folds. Traditionally, the dough was often made with pig's blood to give it some color, and while you're certainly free to try that yourself, I prefer to stick to the vegetables and spices included in this book. You'll have an easier time with this shape if you make the folds over a small wooden dowel, but you can also use a clean pencil. Since this shape is on the smaller side, I prefer to make it in one solid color without using a pattern.

1 batch pasta dough, any color (see chapters 2 and 3)

Semolina flour, for dusting

1. Cut the dough into quarters and work with one piece at a time, leaving the rest covered so it doesn't dry out. Roll the dough to the second- or third-thinnest setting on your pasta machine, or about 1 millimeter thick if rolling by hand.

2. Lightly dust your work surface with flour and lay the pasta sheet down horizontally. Use a sharp knife or pastry roller to cut the sheet into long horizontal strips measuring 2 inches (5 cm) wide. Make diagonal cuts in each strip to create equilateral triangles with sides about 2½ inches (6 cm) long.

3. Cover the triangles with a bowl or kitchen towel so they don't dry out, and work with one piece at a time.

4. Lay a triangle flat in front of you, with one of the sides facing toward you and a point facing away from you. Place a small dowel onto the pasta from the center of the triangle through the middle of the side facing you. The dowel should be pointed toward you.

5. Lift the top tip of the triangle and bend it toward you so it sits flat on the dowel.

6. Holding the tip in place on the dowel, pick up the right tip of the triangle. Bend it toward the center of the triangle so it rests directly on the first tip. Then do the same for the last tip, pressing down so the three tips stick to each other (see Tip).

7. Gently slide the dowel out of the pasta; it should keep its shape.

8. Rest the pasta on a floured surface or piece of parchment paper. Continue with the rest of the dough.

9. Cook the pasta in salted, boiling water until tender, 2 to 5 minutes.

TIP

If the layers don't stick, dab a little water between them to act as glue.

PASTA FACT

Fusi istriani translates to "Istrian spindles," the long rods used to spin wool into yarn. It may have received its name from the wooden dowel we use to bend and shape the dough.

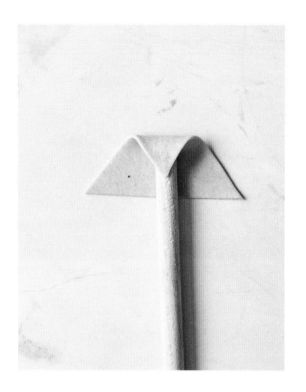
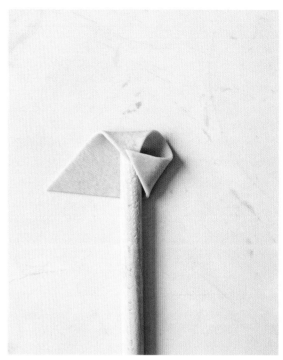

Funghetti

PREP TIME 35 MIN | COOK TIME 5 MIN | 4 to 6 SERVINGS

As you can probably tell by the name, this shape looks like a little mushroom cap, although every time I look at it, I see two big elephant ears (this may have something to do with the fact that my college mascot was Jumbo the Elephant). Either way, this is an easy shape to make, and the rounded sides are great for scooping up sauce. This recipe calls for a circular cookie cutter, but if you don't have one, the top of a wineglass or cup works as well. I like to make this shape with the red and yellow polka dot pattern on page 77, but any pattern or color will do.

1 batch Polka Dots
   (page 77)
Semolina flour, for
   dusting

1. Lightly dust a cutting board with flour and place one sheet of pasta down. Leave the others covered with a kitchen towel so they don't dry out while you're working. Use a cookie cutter or the rim of a glass to cut out 2-inch (5 cm) circles. Remove the scraps and cover them. When you're done, you can knead the scraps back into a dough ball and roll them out to make more pasta.

2. Cover the circles with a bowl or kitchen towel so they don't dry out, and work with one piece at a time.

3. Loosely fold the circle in half, bringing one point on the circle to its exact opposite point. Leave the bottom rounded and do not form a crease.

4. Hold the two points together but do not pinch them shut. The dough should look a bit like a tube. Place the thumb and index finger from your other hand into opposite ends of the tube. Bring these fingers together and pinch the pasta so the two sides stick to each other.

5. The shape should now look like a rounded cone with a stem in the middle.

6. Rest the pasta on a floured surface or piece of parchment paper. Continue with the rest of the dough.

7. Cook the pasta in salted, boiling water until tender, 2 to 5 minutes.

PASTA FACT

There are multiple pasta shapes called *funghetti* or *funghetto*, though they're all a little different. This is a good example of the fact that there's no standard definition for pasta names, so sometimes the same word can refer to many different shapes. More commonly, one shape may have had a dozen different names over time and depending on the region of Italy where it was produced.

Cavatelli

PREP TIME 45 MIN | COOK TIME 5 MIN | 4 to 6 SERVINGS

Cavatelli is the shape that started my entire pasta-making journey. My grandmother used to make it for Christmas dinner every year, so it was the first shape I attempted to make when I couldn't travel home for Christmas one year to see her. It's a simple hand-formed shape that doesn't require a pasta machine or rolling pin, and it's traditionally made with a dough of just flour and water—no eggs. It's best to make these with all OO flour, so they stay soft and supple, and I roll them over my gnocchi board to give them their characteristic ridges. If you don't have a gnocchi board, don't worry—you can use a fork, a slotted spoon, or even a cheese grater to give these little guys some texture!

1 batch All-00 Vegan Dough (page 41) or All-00 Vegan Spinach Dough (page 58)

Semolina flour, for dusting

1. Cut your ball of dough into 8 equal pieces. Cover the dough with a bowl or kitchen towel so it doesn't dry out, and work with one piece at a time.

2. Roll the dough between your hands or on a wooden surface to create a long piece of rope about ½ inch (1 cm) thick (see Tip).

3. Place your dough rope on a cutting board and use a dough scraper or knife to cut it into little squares about ½ inch (1 cm) long.

4. Using a gnocchi board, the back of a fork, a slotted spoon, or a cheese grater, make ridges in the dough. Place each piece of dough on the board, with one of the cut sides facing down. Use your finger to press the dough into the board, then roll down to create ridges. The dough should curl up into a little log, with the ridges on the outside.

5. Rest the pasta on a floured surface or piece of parchment paper. Continue with the rest of the dough.

6. Cook the pasta in salted, boiling water until tender, 2 to 5 minutes.

TIP

If the dough is sticking to your hands or your work surface, sprinkle it with flour.

PASTA FACT

Cavatelli is among the simplest of pasta, just a flour-and-water dough shaped by hand, so it's no surprise that it appears all over Italy with many different names. Some of its close cousins include *capunti, malloreddus, parmatieddi,* and *orecchie di prete.* There are regional differences, like whether you use one finger or two to roll them, what flour is used, and what kind of board they are pressed on.

Sacchetti

PREP TIME 30 MIN | COOK TIME 5 MIN | 4 to 6 SERVINGS

This shape looks like a little bag of filling surrounded by pasta because, well, that's basically what it is. They're also known by the name "beggar's purse," and the filling is kept in place by some strategic dough-pinching. I like to make this shape with Thin Stripes (page 72), but remember that the filling is really the star here, since sacchetti hold a bit more than other shapes.

1 batch filling of choice (see chapter 8)

1 batch Thin Stripes (page 72)

Semolina flour, for dusting

1. Fill a piping bag with filling and cut an opening at the tip about ½ inch (1 cm) wide. If you don't have a piping bag, you can use a spoon.

2. Lightly dust a cutting board with flour and place one sheet of pasta down. Leave the others covered with a kitchen towel so they don't dry out while you're working. Use a sharp knife or a pastry roller to cut the dough into 4-inch (10 cm) squares.

3. Pipe a tablespoon of filling in the center of each square.

4. Lift one corner of the dough straight into the air so it's above the filling. Then grab one of the sides closest to the corner and pull it to the center, pinching the two pieces of dough together right above the filling. Keep working around the square, bringing the edges into the center and pinching them right above the filling. Your goal is to create a seal above the filling so it cannot escape when you cook the pasta. Press firmly around the pinched spot to make sure it's tight, while leaving the tops loose.

5. If you leave these out, even for a short while, the tops will start to droop. If you're not going to cook them right away, place them on a floured sheet pan and stick them in the freezer.

6. Because this shape has a lot of filling and is rather delicate, you'll need to be careful when cooking them so they don't break. Fill a pot with water to cover the height of the pasta shape, add salt, and bring to a boil. Then gently add the pasta to the pot and cook until tender, 2 to 5 minutes. This allows the pasta to stand upright while cooking and not move around too much. You may need to cook these in batches depending on the size of your pot.

PASTA HISTORY

Filled pasta has existed for centuries in cuisines around the world. Although the exact origin of ravioli in Italy is unclear, one of the earliest mentions of a ravioli-type dish is in a collection of Arab recipes by Ibn Butlan, a physician who lived in Baghdad in the 11th century. He wrote about a dish called *sambusaj*, described as triangular pasta filled with ground meat.

Mezzelune

PREP TIME 30 MIN | COOK TIME 5 MIN | 4 to 6 SERVINGS

If you're new to the world of making filled pasta, this is a great shape to start with. It's easy to make and beautiful to look at, with a nice flat surface that proudly shows off colors and designs. But sometimes simple is the most effective, and I like to make these with Classic Pasta Dough (page 38) and a bright filling, like Beet and Goat Cheese Filling (page 231). The beautiful red color of the beets will shine through, making this pasta a stunner. You can cut these with a circular cookie cutter or a wineglass, but using a rounded cookie cutter with scalloped edges makes them particularly beautiful.

1 batch Beet and Goat
  Cheese Filling
  (page 231)

1 batch Classic Pasta
  Dough (page 38)

Semolina flour, for
  dusting

TIPS

1. If the two layers aren't sticking, brush a small amount of water on the dough to act as a glue.

2. If the two layers are coming apart, gently pinch around the edges to seal them.

PASTA FACT

Mezzelune is popular in Northern Italy and into Austria, where it's known as *Schlutzkrapfen* and often served with a spinach and curd filling. In the alpine ski town of Cortina d'Ampezzo, they are known as *casunziei* and are traditionally served with beet filling and a butter-and-poppy seed sauce.

1. Fill a piping bag with filling and cut an opening at the tip about ½ inch (1 cm) wide. If you don't have a piping bag, you can use a spoon.

2. Cut the dough into quarters and work with one piece at a time, leaving the rest covered so it doesn't dry out. Roll the dough to the second- or third-thinnest setting on your pasta machine, or about 1 millimeter thick if rolling by hand.

3. Lightly dust your work surface with flour and place your sheet of pasta on top.

4. Pipe small mounds of filling (about 2 teaspoons) in a row down the center of the pasta sheet about 4 inches (10 cm) apart.

5. Pick up the bottom edge of the pasta sheet and fold it over the filling so the bottom edge meets the top edge. The row of filling should be positioned directly above the crease in the dough.

6. Press down on the dough all around each mound of filling to make sure that the two layers are sealed, doing your best to remove any air bubbles (see Tip 1).

7. Use a sharp knife or a circular cookie cutter about 3 inches (7.5 cm) in diameter to cut out semicircle shapes around each mound of filling (see Tip 2).

8. Place the pasta on a floured surface and continue with the rest of the dough.

9. I recommend cooking mezzelune right away. If you leave it in the fridge, even just for a few hours, the filling can seep into the pasta and make it soggy. If you want to make them ahead of time, place the pieces on a floured baking tray or cutting board and freeze them.

10. Cook the mezzelune in salted boiling water in batches of 10 to 15, depending on the size of your pot. Cook until tender, 2 to 5 minutes, then use a slotted spoon to carefully remove the mezzelune.

Ravioli

PREP TIME 45 MIN | COOK TIME 5 MIN | 4 to 6 SERVINGS

Ravioli is a fun shape to make for three reasons. First, the flat square shape gives you plenty of space to show off your colors and designs. Second, you have the added element of choosing your favorite filling to go inside. Third, and most importantly, you get to eat them—and they're delicious! You can buy ravioli stamps to give you the perfect shape, but I often cut mine freehand. I place the filling in a pastry piping bag to make it easier to work with, but you can use a spoon if you prefer. I use the polka dot technique on page 77 for this shape, but any pattern works well with the large surface area of the ravioli.

1 batch filling of choice (see chapter 8)

1 batch Polka Dots (page 77)

Semolina flour, for dusting

1. Fill a piping bag with filling and cut an opening at the tip about ½ inch (1 cm) wide. If you don't have a piping bag, you can use a spoon.

2. Lightly dust a cutting board with flour and place one sheet of pasta down. Leave the others covered with a kitchen towel so they don't dry out.

3. Pipe small mounds of filling (about 2 teaspoons) in a row on the pasta sheet, with the mounds spaced about 2 inches (5 cm) apart. The row of filling should be about 1 inch (2.5 cm) from the bottom edge of the pasta sheet.

4. Pipe another row of filling about 1 inch (2.5 cm) from the top edge of the pasta sheet.

5. Use a brush or damp paper towel to lightly brush water on the exposed pasta, taking care to get around the mounds of filling. This will make sure the two layers of dough stick together and the ravioli doesn't come apart.

6. Place another sheet of pasta directly on top of the pasta sheet with the filling.

7. Press around the filling with your fingers to remove any air bubbles and to ensure that the two layers are stuck together.

8. If you have a ravioli stamp, press the stamp around each mound of filling to cut out the pasta. Otherwise, use a fluted pastry wheel to cut your ravioli into squares (see Tip 2).

9. Place the ravioli on a floured surface and continue with the rest of the dough.

10. I recommend cooking ravioli right away. If you leave it in the fridge, even just for a few hours, the filling can seep into the pasta and make it soggy. If you want to make ravioli ahead of time, place the pieces on a floured baking tray or cutting board and freeze them.

11. Cook the ravioli in salted boiling water in batches of 10 to 15, depending on the size of your pot. Cook until the pasta is tender, 2 to 5 minutes, then use a slotted spoon to carefully remove them from the pot.

TIPS

1. You can make your ravioli double-sided, with a design on each side, or leave the bottom plain. Sometimes I'll mush together all my pasta scraps, roll them out, and use that as the bottom layer.

2. If you don't have a fluted pastry wheel, you can cut out the ravioli with a sharp knife. Then use a fork to gently press ridges all along the edges of the ravioli squares to prevent the layers from separating.

Tortellini

PREP TIME 45 MIN | COOK TIME 5 MIN | 4 to 6 SERVINGS

I truly believe that a single, well-executed piece of tortellini is one of the most beautiful morsels of food that humans have ever created. The elegant sloping on the sides leading to a commanding point, the bulging pocket stuffed with filling, the dense ring of pasta at the bottom—it all adds up to one delectable bite. Okay, maybe I've lost you, but you have to admit that this classic pasta shape is a great one. Traditional tortellini is filled with meat and served in broth to make *tortellini en brodo*, but you have my permission to use whatever filling and sauce you'd like! With all the folds of tortellini, it can be difficult to see a larger pattern, but this is the perfect shape for some thin, colorful stripes.

1 batch filling of
  choice (see chapter 8)

1 batch Thin Stripes
  (page 72)

Semolina flour, for
  dusting

1. Fill a piping bag with filling and cut an opening at the tip about ½ inch (1 cm) wide. If you don't have a piping bag, you can use a spoon.

2. Lightly dust a cutting board with flour and place one sheet of pasta down. Leave the others covered with a kitchen towel so they don't dry out while you're working. Use a sharp knife or a pastry roller to cut the dough into 2½-inch (6.5 cm) squares.

3. Cover the squares with a bowl or kitchen towel so they don't dry out, and work with one piece at a time.

4. Pipe a small mound of filling (1 to 1½ teaspoons) into the center of the square. Pick up one corner of the dough and fold it over the filling to the opposite corner to make a triangle. Press down on all sides to seal in the filling (see Tip on page 127).

5. Pick up the dough with both hands and place your thumbs on the bottom edge just below the filling. Press up on the center of the bottom edge so the two bottom corners bend downward and start to form a frown. The filling should start to bulge slightly, and a crease should form on either side of it.

6. Move one of your index fingers directly underneath the center of the filling. Bring the two corners toward each other with the thumb and index finger of your opposite hand so the dough starts to wrap around your index finger.

7. Slightly flatten the two corners and bring them together so one sits on top of the other. Press down firmly so they seal together and form one layer of dough (see Tip on page 127).

8. Rest the pasta on a floured surface or piece of parchment paper. Continue with the rest of the dough.

9. Cook the pasta in salted, boiling water until tender, 2 to 5 minutes.

TIP

You may need to brush a little water on the dough to act as a glue if the layers are not sticking.

PASTA HISTORY

Various Italian cities claim to be the birthplace of tortellini, but one legend has it that the Roman goddess Venus once stayed at a hotel where the innkeeper was so taken by her beauty that he created a pasta shape in honor of her belly button. That pasta, *l'ombelico di Venere*, is what we now call tortellini.

Cestini

PREP TIME 50 MIN | COOK TIME 5 MIN | 4 to 6 SERVINGS

Cestini means "baskets" in Italian, a fitting name for these little pouches of filling that look a bit like a crab rangoon. The shape is simple yet elegant, with a few pinches here and there encapsulating the filling and creating a starlike shape that looks like a more refined version of Sacchetti (page 118). I think these look great with the Classic Pasta Dough (page 38), since the yellowish color complements the star shape, but feel free to use any color you like.

1 batch filling of choice (see chapter 8)

1 batch Classic Pasta Dough (page 38)

Semolina flour, for dusting

1. Fill a piping bag with filling and cut an opening at the tip about ½ inch (1 cm) wide. If you don't have a piping bag, you can use a spoon.

2. Cut the dough into quarters and work with one piece at a time, leaving the rest covered so it doesn't dry out. Roll the dough to the second- or third-thinnest setting on your pasta machine, or about 1 millimeter thick if rolling by hand.

3. Lightly dust a cutting board with flour. Use a sharp knife or a pastry roller to cut the dough into 4-inch (10 cm) squares.

4. Pipe a dollop of filling (1 to 1½ teaspoons) in the center of each square.

5. Lift two opposite corners of the square up and over the filling, then press them together to make a point.

6. Lift one of the remaining corners up over the filling and toward the center. The sides of that corner piece should meet the sides of the already-folded dough. Press the edges together to seal the dough and ensure that no filling escapes.

7. Repeat with the remaining corner, doing your best to press out any air before the filling is fully encapsulated.

8. Give all the seams one final press to make sure the filling is sealed inside.

9. Rest the pasta on a floured surface or piece of parchment paper. Continue with the rest of the dough.

10. Cook the pasta in boiling, salted water until tender, 2 to 5 minutes.

PASTA HISTORY

Although we now think of both ravioli and tortellini as filled pastas, that wasn't always the case. An Italian dictionary published in 1612 by the Accademia della Crusca differentiates between *raviolo*, the filling, and *tortello*, "a kind of *raviolo* with pasta wrapping." Depending on the region and the time period, the word ravioli can refer to the entire filled pasta or just the filling.

Ravioli Al'Uovo

PREP TIME 25 MIN | COOK TIME 5 MIN | 4 to 6 SERVINGS

This is a pasta with a wow factor: Individual egg yolks sit in a nest of filling, so when you cut into them, the runny yolks mix with the cheese filling and the sauce to make a rich, decadent bite. It requires a gentle touch so you don't break the yolk or rip the pasta, but the steps are straightforward and the payoff is big. It's also the perfect dish to show off your new pattern-making skills because it has such a large surface area. Using Flower- and Herb-Laminated Dough (page 92) is particularly elegant. You can use any filling or sauce you want, but I like to make these with Spinach–Ricotta Filling (page 224) and Brown Butter with Toasted Hazelnuts and Sage (page 184) for extra richness.

1 batch Spinach-Ricotta Filling (page 224)

½ batch Classic Pasta Dough (page 38)

½ batch Flower- and Herb-Laminated Dough (page 92)

12 egg yolks

Semolina flour, for dusting

1. Fill a piping bag with filling and cut an opening at the tip about ¾ inch (2 cm) wide. If you don't have a piping bag, you can use a spoon.

2. Cut the classic dough in half and work with one piece at a time, leaving the other covered so it doesn't dry out. Roll the dough to the second- or third-thinnest setting on your pasta machine, or about 1 millimeter thick if rolling by hand. The pasta sheet should be about 22 inches (56 cm) long.

3. Lightly dust your work surface with flour and place the pasta sheet on top.

4. Pipe a thick line of filling in a circle about 2 inches (5 cm) from the left edge of the pasta sheet and 2 inches (5 cm) from the bottom edge. The circle should be slightly larger than the size of an egg yolk. If you're using a spoon, place a big dollop on each center point and make an indentation in the middle where the yolk will go.

5. Pipe another circle of filling 3 inches (7.5 cm) directly to the right of your first circle. Then continue piping circles in the same row, each 3 inches (7.5 cm) apart. You should be able to fit five to six circles on one sheet of pasta (see Tip on page 133).

6. Gently place a yolk in the center of each filling circle.

7. Use a brush or paper towel to lightly brush water onto the dough surrounding the filling.

8. Place a sheet of the herb-laminated pasta directly on top of the original pasta sheet.

9. Press on the dough all around the filling to tightly seal the two layers, being careful to remove any air bubbles.

10. You can use a cookie cutter to cut these into circles, but I prefer to use a fluted pastry roller to cut them into large, 3- to 4-inch (7.5 to 10 cm) squares.

PASTA HISTORY

This dish originated at the two-Michelin-starred restaurant San Domenico, outside Bologna, in the 1970s, and it's still on the menu today. It's served with a spinach-ricotta filling and a butter, truffle oil, and sage sauce.

11. Place the ravioli on a floured surface and continue with the rest of the dough.

12. Cook the ravioli immediately in a large pot of boiling salted water. Cook in batches of two to three at a time, so they don't break while cooking. Cook them just enough for the pasta to be tender, 3 to 4 minutes, but not so long that the yolks are no longer runny.

TIP

It's fine to use a smaller sheet of pasta and make fewer than five ravioli at a time. Just make sure the circles of filling are spaced about 3 inches (7.5 cm) apart.

PASTA HISTORY

In 1924, an Italian immigrant named Ettore Boiardi opened a restaurant in Cleveland and began selling jars of his pasta sauce to customers. They were so popular that he started selling the sauce full time. He created a line of ready-to-cook meals that contained uncooked spaghetti, sauce, and grated cheese and eventually produced rations for the United States Army during World War II. You may know him by his Americanized name, Chef Boyardee.

Caramelle

PREP TIME 45 MIN | COOK TIME 5 MIN | 4 to 6 SERVINGS

A 2018 *Grub Street* article called caramelle the "hottest new pasta shape," and it's easy to see why. This stuffed pasta looks just like an old-fashioned piece of candy—think of the butterscotch candy your grandmother used to give you, or perhaps a piece of saltwater taffy—making it the perfect shape to show off your colorful dough. A striped caramelle always looks beautiful, but if you're feeling ambitious, I love the look of Spirals (page 81) lined up perfectly with the center of the pasta.

1 batch Spirals
  (page 81)

1 batch filling of
  choice (see chapter 8)

Semolina flour, for
  dusting

1. Fill a piping bag with filling and cut an opening at the tip about ½ inch (1 cm) wide. If you don't have a piping bag, you can use a spoon.

2. Lightly dust a cutting board with flour and set the spiral circles down. Use a sharp knife or a pastry roller to cut them into 3 × 2-inch (7.5 × 5 cm) rectangles (see Tip 1 on page 137).

3. Cover the pieces with a bowl or kitchen towel so they don't dry out, and work with one piece at a time.

4. Starting ½ inch (1 cm) from the left edge of the pasta rectangle, pipe a line of filling horizontally across, about ½ inch (1 cm) from the bottom edge, stopping ¼ inch (6 mm) from the right edge.

5. Lift the bottom edge of the pasta and fold it over the filling, tucking it under slightly (see Tip 2 on page 137). Then roll the filled section one more time so your pasta looks like a tube.

6. Press down on either side of the filling with one finger to seal it in place, but don't press down all the way to the ends.

7. Pinch the pressed-down dough on either side of the filling to create a candy shape. Gently fan out the edges of the dough so they look like candy wrappers.

8. Rest the pasta on a floured surface or piece of parchment paper. Continue with the rest of the dough.

9. Cook the pasta in salted, boiling water until tender, 2 to 5 minutes.

PASTA FACT

The origins of caramelle are unclear, but in the last decade or so, they've popped up on numerous Italian restaurant menus in the United States. They are most likely a newer creation, but they may have been adapted from *tortelli piacentini*, a filled pasta with a little tail served in the Emilia-Romagna region of Northern Italy.

TIPS

1. If you're using a regular sheet of pasta, cut it into 3 × 2-inch (7.5 × 5 cm) rectangles. I like to use a fluted pastry wheel to cut the short end and a regular pastry wheel to cut the long end, but if you don't have those, a regular knife is fine.

2. If your dough is dry, brush a small amount of water on the remaining flat part that sticks out above your rolled-up filling.

CHAPTER SIX

New Shapes

Sometimes, when I make pasta, my daughter sits at the kitchen counter next to me. I give her a ball of dough and my hand-crank pasta machine, and she'll turn it over and over, flattening the dough, smushing it up into a ball, and flattening it again. Eventually she'll ask me to move the crank to the fettuccine cutter, and she'll cut the dough into chunky, uneven strips. One time, my husband walked into the kitchen, and she looked up at him with a big grin, held up the pile of dough in her hand, and said, "I'm making pasta like Daddy D!"

Becoming a dad was the greatest thing I've ever done, and I've loved watching my daughter grow from a newborn to an infant to a toddler. When my grandmother passed away right after my first Christmas as a parent, I began to think a lot about family and traditions, and the values and insights that I wanted to pass on to my daughter. My family had a lot of traditions growing up, for the holidays and other times of year, and I found comfort in these rituals and a sense of belonging in knowing that I'd be doing the same things, with the same group of people, every year. Now my husband and I are blending our family traditions and making new ones for our daughter. In some ways, the exact foods we eat or the traditions we keep don't matter so much; it's about instilling in my daughter the knowledge that she is loved, cherished, and part of something bigger than herself.

It probably won't surprise you that some of our new traditions involve pasta, and we already started last year with the addition of decorating Christmas Tree Ravioli (page 169) alongside my family tradition of decorating cookies. This chapter is all about creating something new, as it contains recipes for 17 pasta shapes you might not have seen before. The inspiration for these shapes came from all over: traditional pastas, the world of baking, other talented pasta artists, or sometimes a far-off place in my imagination. For each recipe, I include colors and patterns that I think work well together, but feel free to experiment with others!

Four-Petal Flowers

PREP TIME 45 MIN | COOK TIME 5 MIN | 4 to 6 SERVINGS

I debated whether to call this shape a flower or a butterfly. Depending on how I look at it, I can see either one, and maybe you'll see something else entirely. But no matter what you call it, it's certainly a beautiful shape, with four little bowls that are perfect for collecting sauce. I like to put a few of these in broth for a quick soup and watch as the steamy liquid fills up the petals. These are basically two Funghetti (page 114) fused together, so if you've mastered that shape, this one should be no problem. I make these with a solid color, but feel free to use a pattern if you prefer.

1 batch pasta dough, any color (see chapters 2 and 3)

Semolina flour, for dusting

1. Cut the dough into quarters and work with one piece at a time, leaving the rest covered so it doesn't dry out. Roll out a sheet of dough to the second- or third-thinnest setting on your pasta machine, or about 1 millimeter thick if rolling by hand.

2. Lightly dust a cutting board with flour. Use a circular cookie cutter or the top of a shot glass to cut the dough into 1½-inch (4 cm) circles.

3. Cover the circles with a bowl or kitchen towel so they don't dry out, and work with two pieces at a time.

4. Loosely fold one circle in half, bringing one point on the edge of the circle to its exact opposite point. Leave the bottom rounded and do not form a crease. Pinch the two points together so they stick and the pasta looks like a little tube. Place the thumb and index finger from your other hand into opposite ends of the tube. Bring these fingers together and pinch the pasta so the two sides stick to each other. Repeat with the other circle.

5. Place the two shapes next to each other so the flatter sides of each one are touching. Pinch these sides together so they stick, so the pasta looks like four circles fused together. Give each conjoining side a nice pinch to make sure the circles are stuck together.

6. Rest the pasta on a floured surface or piece of parchment paper. Continue with the rest of the dough.

7. Cook in salted, boiling water until tender, 2 to 5 minutes.

PASTA HISTORY

In the 1500s, Neapolitan pasta makers developed machines to manufacture their pasta, but they faced the problem of how to quickly dry the pasta to make it last longer. To solve this, the pasta makers would carry freshly made pasta on large racks through the streets to find the perfect wind for drying.

Long Farfalle

PREP TIME 35 MIN | COOK TIME 5 MIN | 4 to 6 SERVINGS

I make this shape quite a lot, because it's perfect for showing off colors and patterns. It's a variation of the traditional Farfalle (page 107) shape, but its long, elegant body can fit more stripes than almost any other shape in this book. Use this shape to show off an entire rainbow of doughs, or make ombre pasta using four or five doughs in varying hues of the same color. You'll end up with a lot more scraps than with traditional farfalle; be sure to save them to make some Tie-Dye pasta (page 84)!

1 batch Ombre Pasta dough (page 71)

Semolina flour, for dusting

1. Lightly dust a cutting board with flour and place one pasta sheet down horizontally. Leave the others covered with a kitchen towel so they don't dry out while you're working.

2. Use a sharp knife or pastry roller to cut out long, pointy ovals that extend from the top edge of the pasta sheet to the bottom edge. They should be about 6 inches (15 cm) long and about 1½ inches (4 cm) at the widest point in the center. Remove the excess dough.

3. Cover the ovals with a bowl or kitchen towel so they don't dry out, and work with one piece at a time.

4. Lay an oval flat on your work surface. Place your thumb and index finger on either side of the oval at the widest point. Use your other hand to keep the center point of the oval flat on your work surface while you slowly pinch. A ridge should form on either side of the flat center. Press the ridges together until they stick (see Tips).

5. Rest the pasta on a floured surface or piece of parchment paper. Continue with the rest of the dough.

6. Cook the pasta in boiling, salted water until tender, 2 to 5 minutes.

PASTA FACT

Although this oval shape may not be so traditional, you can sometimes find a larger version of farfalle called *farfalloni*, or a miniature version called *farfalline*, in stores.

TIPS

1. If the ridges aren't sticking together, use your finger to brush a tiny amount of water between them to act as a glue.

2. If you're having trouble getting the folds just right, place a thin skewer vertically down the middle of your oval. This will keep the center in place while you squeeze the two sides together so they stick. When you pull the skewer out, the folds should stay in place.

Sunflowers

PREP TIME 60 MIN | COOK TIME 7 MIN | 6 to 8 SERVINGS

Back when I was a law student living in New York City, I couldn't afford much, but one of my favorite little luxuries was stopping by a flower stand on the Upper West Side and picking up a bunch of sunflowers. As I sat hunched over my law books, it always made me happy to look up and see their yellow faces staring back at me. Granted, the moment of joy was fleeting because I usually had about 100 more pages of reading to do, but I appreciated it all the same. These sunflower ravioli can be made with Classic Pasta Dough (page 38) or Turmeric Pasta Dough (page 54) for a brighter yellow color, and with a little Brown Pasta Dough (page 65) for the center.

1 batch filling of choice (see chapter 8)

1 batch Classic Pasta Dough (page 38) or Turmeric Pasta Dough (page 54)

¼ batch Brown Pasta Dough (page 65, see Note)

Semolina flour, for dusting

1. Fill a piping bag with filling and cut an opening at the tip about ½ inch (1 cm) wide. If you don't have a piping bag, you can use a spoon.

2. Divide the classic dough into quarters and work with one piece at a time, leaving the rest covered so it doesn't dry out. Roll the dough to the second- or third-thinnest setting on your pasta machine, or about 1 millimeter thick if rolling by hand.

3. Dust a cutting board with flour, then place the pasta sheet on top. Use a circular cookie cutter or the top of a wineglass to make an imprint of a 3½-inch (9 cm) circle on the dough, but don't cut all the way through. Make a line of 5 to 6 circles down the sheet of pasta.

4. Pipe a tablespoon of filling in the center of each circle.

5. Place another sheet of pasta on top (see Tip). Be careful not to form any air bubbles. Press around the filling to make sure that the layers stick together.

6. To make the pile of filling as neat as possible, use the dull side of a 1½-inch (4 cm) circular cookie cutter or the top of a shot glass and place it around the filling. Press down gently to create a clearly defined bubble of filling in the center.

7. Roll out the brown dough to the thinnest setting on your pasta machine, or as thin as you can if rolling by hand.

8. Use a circular cookie cutter or the top of a shot glass to make 1½-inch (4 cm) circles of brown dough.

9. Use a fork to poke dents all over one side of the brown circles to make the sunflower seeds. Don't poke all the way through.

10. Brush a small amount of water on the center of each ravioli, then place the brown circles on top so they stick.

TIP

If your pasta has dried out, brush the first layer with a small amount of water to act as a glue between the layers.

11. Use a fork to press lines all the way around the rim of the circle. The lines should be about ¾ inch (2 cm) long but not reach the filling. You should be able to make 9 or 10 fork prints around the circle.

12. Cut out small triangles about ¾ inch (2 cm) long between each fork print. This will leave you with a jagged edge that looks like a series of mountains with flat tops.

13. Pinch the end of each mountaintop to create a point.

14. Set the sunflower on a floured surface and continue with the rest of the dough.

15. I recommend cooking these right away. If you leave them in the fridge, even just for a few hours, the filling can seep into the pasta and make it soggy. If you want to make them ahead of time, place the pieces on a floured baking tray or cutting board and freeze them.

16. Cook the sunflowers in salted boiling water in batches of 10 to 15, depending on the size of your pot. Cook each batch until the pasta is tender, 4 to 7 minutes, then use a slotted spoon to carefully remove the sunflowers. Repeat until all the pasta has been cooked.

NOTE

If you leave off the brown circles, you'll have little ravioli suns instead of sunflowers!

Candy

PREP TIME 35 MIN | COOK TIME 5 MIN | 4 to 6 SERVINGS

One of my favorite parts of going to the Jersey Shore as a kid was the trip to the candy store, and I still keep a well-stocked drawer of sweets at my house. So it should come as no surprise that this is the second candy-shaped pasta in this book. The origin of this shape is pretty simple: One day, when I was making Farfalle (page 107), I decided to pinch the dough twice instead of once. After playing around a bit, I developed something that looks quite a bit like Caramelle (page 134) without the filling. These look great with a solid-colored dough, but I love the way they look filled with colorful abstract lines.

1 batch Abstract Lines dough (page 78)

Semolina flour, for dusting

1. Lightly dust a cutting board with flour and place one pasta sheet down. Leave the others covered with a kitchen towel so they don't dry out while you're working. Use a sharp knife or a pastry roller to cut the dough into rectangles of about 3 × 1½ inches (7.5 × 4 cm). I like to use a fluted pastry wheel to cut the short end and a regular pastry wheel to cut the long end, but a regular knife works fine, too.

2. Cover the rectangles with a bowl or kitchen towel so they don't dry out, and work with one piece at a time.

3. Hold the rectangle vertically with both hands and place your thumbs on top, as if you're very loosely holding your phone to text someone. Pinch the sides of the dough about ½ inch (1 cm) from the bottom edge while using your thumbs to hold the center of the dough in place. This should create two ridges in the dough on either side of the middle of the rectangle. Press the two ridges together until they stick (see Tips).

4. Rotate the dough so the pinched end is on top. Then follow the same method to make another pinch about ½ inch (1 cm) from the bottom edge.

5. Use your fingers to gently round out the center of the shape to form a bowl.

6. Rest the pasta on a floured surface or piece of parchment paper. Continue with the rest of the dough.

7. Cook the pasta in boiling, salted water until tender, 2 to 5 minutes.

PASTA HISTORY

The first pasta factory in the United States was opened in 1848 in Brooklyn by Antoine Zerega, a French immigrant whose family was originally from Northern Italy. Brooklyn eventually became a major producer of pasta thanks to the influx of Italian immigrants and a halt in trading with Europe during the First World War.

TIPS

1. If the ridges aren't sticking together, use your finger to brush a tiny amount of water between them to act as a glue.

2. If you're having trouble getting the folds just right, place a thin skewer vertically down the middle of your rectangle. This will keep the center in place while you squeeze the two sides together so they stick. When you pull the skewer out, the folds should stay in place.

Pinwheels

PREP TIME 25 MIN | COOK TIME 5 MIN | 4 to 6 SERVINGS

I've spent a lot of time in my life at the beach, from vacations at the Jersey Shore as a kid to the year my husband, Steve, and I spent living in Sunset Beach, North Carolina, after our daughter was born. I always associate pinwheels with the ocean, whirling away outside a toy store on the boardwalk or spinning in the breeze on someone's front porch. While pinwheel pasta doesn't have quite as much motion as the real thing, it's a playful, fun, and tasty shape. I like to use two different colored doughs and flatten them into one sheet of pasta so the bottom color peeks through when folding the dough.

½ batch Pink Pasta Dough (page 64)

½ batch Classic Pasta Dough (page 38)

Semolina flour, for dusting

1. Divide the pink dough in half and leave one half covered so it doesn't dry out. Roll the dough to the thinnest setting on your pasta machine, or as thin as you can if rolling by hand. Lay it down on a piece of parchment paper or floured surface. Repeat this step with the classic pasta dough.

2. Carefully place the sheet of classic pasta dough directly on top of the pink one. Remove any air bubbles by gently pushing the air to the edge of the pasta sheet (see Tip 1).

3. Roll the double-sided sheet of pasta through your pasta machine to the second- or third-thinnest setting, or about 1 millimeter thick if rolling by hand.

4. Dust a cutting board with flour, then place the sheet on top. Use a sharp knife or a pastry roller to cut the dough into 4-inch (10 cm) squares.

5. Cover the squares with a bowl or kitchen towel so they don't dry out, and work with one piece at a time.

6. Cut a diagonal line from one corner of the square directly toward the middle, stopping about ½ inch (1 cm) from the center point. Do this with the other three corners so you have four cuts that do not touch each other.

7. Starting with the top left corner, pick up the tip of dough to the right of the cut and carefully bend it up and over toward the middle of the square. Press only the tip of the dough into the center of the square so that it sticks into place. The rest of the folded dough should be rounded, like a pinwheel.

8. Move to the top right corner. Pick up the tip of the dough to the right of the cut and bend it up and over toward the center, pressing in the tip securely. Repeat for the remaining two corners. Use a knife to give each of the four points of the pinwheel a rounded tip.

9. Use a knife or cookie cutter to cut out a ½-inch (1 cm) circle of dough and place it in the center of the pinwheel.

TIPS

1. If the two layers aren't sticking together, brush a small amount of water in between them to act as a glue.

2. The rounded pieces will start to droop if you leave the pinwheels out for too long, so either cook them immediately or place them on a floured surface and freeze.

10. Rest the pasta on a floured surface or piece of parchment paper. Continue with the rest of the dough.

11. Cook in salted, boiling water until tender, 2 to 5 minutes.

PASTA HISTORY

In the 1960s, Italy passed a "pasta purity" law that required all commercial pasta to be made with durum wheat. Foreign manufacturers sued to block the law, leading to what the press called the Pasta Wars. When the law was eventually overturned, a local newspaper declared that "Italians will have to say goodbye to their beloved firm pasta," which would be replaced by "gluey and insipid pasta" from Germany. Those fears appear to have been overblown.

Rose Ravioli

PREP TIME 45 MIN | COOK TIME 10 MIN | 6 to 8 SERVINGS

These roses might be perfect for Valentine's Day, but there's no reason why you can't make them all year long. After all, who doesn't love being surprised with a dozen roses, especially when they're edible and filled with cheese! You can customize these roses with whatever filling, color, and pattern you'd like, but my favorite is the deep pink Beet Pasta Dough (page 50).

1 batch filling of choice (see chapter 8)

1 batch Beet Pasta Dough (page 50)

Semolina flour, for dusting

1. Fill a piping bag with filling and cut an opening at the tip about ¾ inch (2 cm) wide. If you don't have a piping bag, you can use a spoon.

2. Divide the dough into quarters and work with one piece at a time, leaving the rest covered so it doesn't dry out. Roll out a sheet of dough to the thinnest or second-thinnest setting on your pasta machine, or about 1 millimeter thick if rolling by hand.

3. Lightly dust a cutting board with flour. Use a cookie cutter or the top of a wineglass to cut the dough into 3-inch (7.5 cm) circles.

4. Lay four circles next to each other in a row but have them overlap by about 50 percent.

5. Starting about ½ inch (1 cm) from the left end of the circles, pipe a row of filling across the center, stopping about ½ inch (1 cm) from the right side.

6. Pick up the bottom edge of the circles and fold it up over the filling so it's even with the top edge. Press down firmly around the filling so it doesn't leak out, making sure not to leave any air bubbles (see Tip 1).

7. Rotate the pasta 90 degrees, so it's vertical on your surface. Lift the bottom edge and roll the pasta as if you're rolling up a sleeping bag (see Tip 2).

8. Use a small amount of water to seal the top end onto the pasta roll so it doesn't unroll.

9. Your rose should now stand up on its own. Set the rose on a floured surface and continue with the rest of the dough.

10. To cook, bring a pot of salted water to a boil and cook until the bottom layer is cooked through, 8 to 10 minutes.

TIPS

1. If your two layers aren't sticking together, brush a little water in between them to act as a glue.

2. If you've used too much filling, this might be difficult, but it's okay to roll the pasta up a little more loosely.

FOOD FACT

Italians have been known to use flowers in their cooking, perhaps most famously in the dish *fiori di zucca fritti*. Fresh zucchini blossoms are stuffed with ricotta (or left plain), dipped in a flour batter, and fried and served during the summer as an appetizer or street food.

Cookie Cutter Ravioli

PREP TIME 45 MIN | COOK TIME 5 MIN | 6 to 8 SERVINGS

Cookie cutters are the pasta tool you never knew you needed but won't be able to live without. If you think about it, what is a traditional ravioli stamp but a cookie cutter with jagged edges? Cookie cutters allow you to make virtually endless pasta shapes. Pasta penguins? Ravioli rodents? Stars? Hearts? Letters? Numbers? You can find a cookie cutter for almost any shape you can think of, so get a few of your favorites and start cooking.

1 batch filling of choice (see chapter 8)

1 batch pasta dough, any color (see chapters 2 and 3)

Semolina flour, for dusting

1. Fill a piping bag with filling and cut an opening at the tip about ½ inch (1 cm) wide. If you don't have a piping bag, you can use a spoon.

2. Divide the dough into quarters and work with one piece at a time, leaving the rest covered so it doesn't dry out. Roll out a sheet of dough to the second- or third-thinnest setting on your pasta machine, or about 1 millimeter thick if rolling by hand.

3. Dust a cutting board with flour, then place the pasta sheet on top. Make a light imprint of the cookie cutter on the dough, without going all the way through. Repeat this over the entire sheet of dough.

4. Pipe filling into the middle of the outline of each shape. Do not overfill or get too close to the edges, or the filling will seep out when you cook it.

5. Use a brush, a paper towel, or your finger to lightly brush water on the dough around the filling to help the two layers of the ravioli stick together.

6. Roll out another sheet of pasta dough and place it directly on top of the first layer. Press all around the filling to make sure the layers stick together and to remove any air bubbles.

7. Cut out the shapes by pressing down on the dough swiftly but firmly around each pile of filling with the cookie cutter, making sure the filling isn't too close to any of the edges. Remove the excess dough.

8. Inspect each ravioli and pinch together any loose parts around the edges.

9. Set the ravioli on a floured surface and continue with the rest of the dough.

10. I recommend cooking ravioli right away. If you leave it in the fridge, even just for a few hours, the filling can seep into the pasta and make it soggy. If you want to make ravioli ahead of time, place the pieces on a floured baking tray or cutting board and freeze them.

11. Cook the ravioli in salted boiling water in batches of 10 to 15, depending on the size of your pot. Cook each batch until tender, 2 to 5 minutes, then use a slotted spoon to carefully remove the ravioli. Repeat until all the pasta has been cooked.

NOTE

The main concern with using cookie cutters is that the pasta won't hold in the filling well enough or it'll burst when you cook it. A traditional ravioli stamp has jagged edges to prevent this from happening, but I've provided some extra steps to keep your cookie cutter ravioli perfectly intact.

Succulent Ravioli

PREP TIME 60 MIN | COOK TIME 10 MIN | 6 to 8 SERVINGS

I was walking through a craft store one day when a little tool for cake decorating caught my eye. It was a stencil for making mini succulents out of fondant, and I immediately thought, *I could use that to make pasta*. My husband Steve later suggested I add a layer of orange dough to the bottom, to make it look like the plants were sitting in little terracotta pots, and my succulent ravioli was born. To help you replicate the shape, I've provided a stencil on page 163. You can try to recreate this freehand, using a knife, or trace the outline onto a piece of cardboard, cut it out, and then trace that on your pasta dough. The recipe below uses Spinach Pasta Dough (page 57), but I also make these with Mint Green Pasta Dough (page 65) and Beet Pasta Dough (page 50).

1 batch filling of choice (see chapter 8)

1 batch Spinach Pasta Dough (page 57)

½ batch Roasted Red Pepper Pasta Dough (page 53)

Semolina flour, for dusting

TIPS

1. If your pasta has started to dry out, lightly brush a small amount of water in between the layers to help them stay sealed.

2. If you've used too much filling, this might be difficult, but it's okay to roll the pasta up a little more loosely.

PASTA FACT

Flowers and plants are a common inspiration for pasta shapes, such as *gigli*, meaning "lilies," *fiori*, meaning "flowers," and *foglie di oliva*, meaning "olive leaves."

1. Fill a piping bag with filling and cut an opening at the tip about ¾ inch (2 cm) wide. If you don't have a piping bag, you can use a spoon.

2. Trace the succulent stencil onto a thin piece of cardboard (a cereal box works great) and cut it out.

3. Divide the green dough into quarters and work with one piece at a time, leaving the rest covered so it doesn't dry out. Roll out a sheet of dough to the third-thinnest setting on your pasta machine, or about 1 millimeter thick if rolling by hand.

4. Dust a cutting board with flour, then place the green pasta sheet on top. Dust the pasta sheet with flour, then place the stencil on the dough and use a sharp paring knife or X-Acto knife to cut out the shape.

5. Place the cut-out shape horizontally in front of you. Starting about ½ inch (1 cm) from the left side, pipe a thick line of filling across the center of the shape, stopping about ½ inch (1 cm) from the right side.

6. Pick up the bottom spikes and fold them around the filling until the tips are even with the top spikes. The spikes should be staggered and not overlap with each other completely.

7. Press around the filling to make sure it's completely sealed (see Tip 1).

8. Rotate the pasta so that it's vertical and the spikes are facing right. Carefully lift up the bottom edge and roll the pasta as if you're rolling up a sleeping bag (see Tip 2).

9. Use a small amount of water to seal the top end onto the pasta roll so it doesn't unroll.

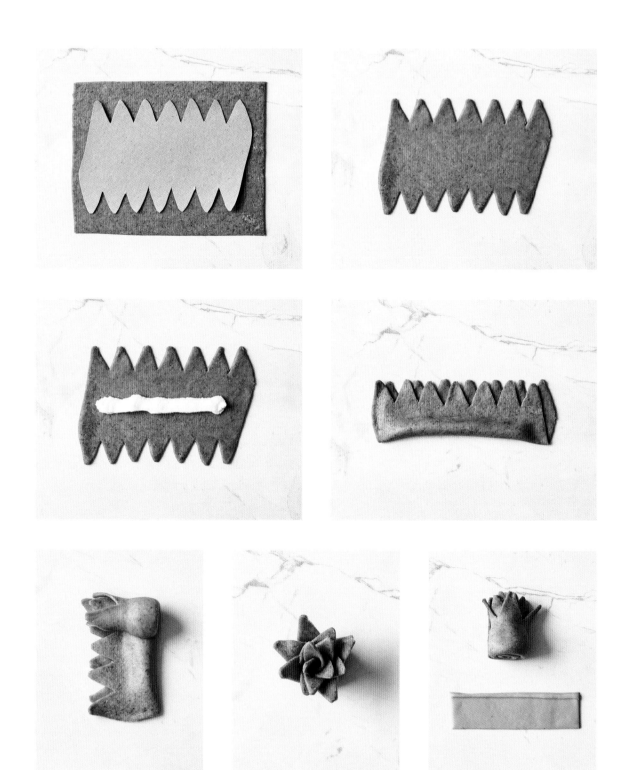

10. Place the succulent on a piece of parchment paper or floured surface. It should be able to stand up on its own. Gently pull down the spikes and fan them out to create leaves.

11. Divide the orange dough in half and leave one piece covered. Roll out the other piece to the thinnest setting on your pasta machine, or as thin as you can roll it by hand.

12. Place the orange dough on the floured cutting board. Cut a 3½ × 1-inch (9 × 2.5 cm) rectangle. Then cut a 3½ × ⅛-inch (9 cm × 3 mm) strip.

13. Place the strip on top of the larger rectangle right along the top edge; this will be the lip of the pot. Press down slightly so it sticks.

14. If your succulent is dry, rub around the stem with a damp paper towel or brush. Then wrap the orange rectangle around the stem of the succulent until it reaches all the way around. You may need to stretch it a little bit or cut off any excess if it's too long.

15. Set the succulent on a floured surface and continue with the rest of the dough.

16. The succulents require some special care while cooking, because the base is so much denser than the leaves. Fill a wide pan with water about 1½ inches (4 cm) high. Add a spoonful of salt and bring to a boil. Place each succulent in the water and let them cook until the bottom is fully cooked through, 8 to 10 minutes. This allows the fully submerged base to cook completely while the leaves cook from the steam. Nudge the succulents every few minutes so they don't stick to the bottom.

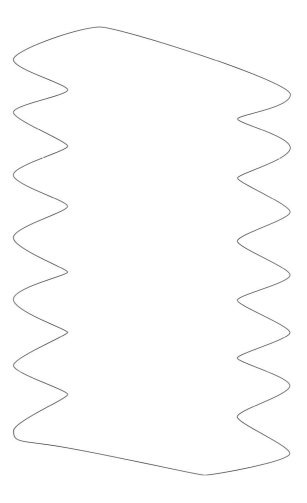

STENCIL

Trace this stencil onto a thin piece of cardboard.

Chocolate Chip Cookie Ravioli

PREP TIME 45 MIN | COOK TIME 5 MIN | 6 to 8 SERVINGS

Requests for cookie ravioli have become so common at our house that I always try to keep a batch of them in the freezer. My two-year-old daughter knows they're not actually cookies, of course, but something about a dinner in the shape of her second-favorite food absolutely delights her (pasta is her favorite, obviously!). I use whole wheat flour for this recipe, to give the ravioli the color of a well-baked chocolate chip cookie, but Classic Pasta Dough (page 38) would work fine, too. I also use a small amount of cocoa dough for the chocolate chips, but you could easily swap that out for any other color—they could be sprinkle cookies instead!

1 batch filling of choice (see chapter 8)

1 batch Whole Wheat Classic Pasta Dough (page 38)

¼ batch Brown Pasta Dough (page 65)

Semolina flour, for dusting

1. Fill a piping bag with filling and cut an opening at the tip about ½ inch (1 cm) wide. If you don't have a piping bag, you can use a spoon.

2. Divide the whole wheat dough into quarters and work with one piece at a time, leaving the rest covered so it doesn't dry out. Roll out a sheet of dough to the second- or third-thinnest setting on your pasta machine, or about 1 millimeter thick if rolling by hand.

3. Dust a cutting board with flour, then place the whole wheat pasta sheet on top.

4. Use a 3-inch (7.5 cm) circular cookie cutter or the top of a wineglass to lightly press a circle into the dough, but don't cut all the way through. Make a line of 7 to 8 circles down the sheet of pasta.

5. Pipe a dollop of filling (1 to 1½ tablespoons) into each circle. Place the filling slightly off center, so one side of the circle has no filling in it.

6. Use a brush, a paper towel, or your finger to lightly brush water onto the dough around the filling, to help the two layers of the ravioli stick together.

7. Roll out another quarter of the whole wheat dough, then place it directly on top of the first layer. Press all around the filling to make sure the layers stick together and to remove any air bubbles.

8. Use your cookie cutter to cut circles into the dough around each dollop of filling. Remove the excess dough.

9. Press down on the side of the circle with no filling to make sure the layers are fused together. Then use a sharp paring knife or X-Acto knife to cut out the shape of a bite mark.

10. Roll the brown dough to the thinnest setting on your pasta machine, or as thin as you can roll it by hand.

11. To make the chocolate chips, use a sharp paring knife or X-Acto knife to cut small triangles, squares, and other shapes out of the brown dough. They should look like baked chocolate chips, so they don't need to be perfect!

12. Use a brush, a paper towel, or your finger to brush a small amount of water on the top of your cookie ravioli to act as a glue. Place your chocolate chips onto the cookies and press down gently so they stick.

13. Set the ravioli on a floured surface and continue with the rest of the dough.

14. I recommend cooking ravioli right away. If you leave it in the fridge, even just for a few hours, the filling can seep into the pasta and make it soggy. If you want to make ravioli ahead of time, place the pieces on a floured baking tray or cutting board and freeze them.

15. Cook the ravioli in salted boiling water in batches of 10 to 15, depending on the size of your pot. Cook until tender, 2 to 5 minutes, then use a slotted spoon to carefully remove the ravioli. Repeat until all the pasta has been cooked.

(Real) Brown Butter Chocolate Chip Cookies

My husband insisted I find a way to include my recipe for actual chocolate chip cookies in the book, and this seems like the right spot for it!

1 cup (225 g) unsalted butter

1½ cups (300 g) packed brown sugar

¼ cup (50 g) granulated sugar

2 eggs

1 tablespoon vanilla extract

2¼ cups (270 g) all-purpose flour

1 teaspoon baking soda

½ teaspoon salt

1½ cups (250 g) chocolate chips

1. Melt the butter in a saucepan over medium heat. Stir occasionally as the butter bubbles up, the foaming begins to subside, and brown bits appear on the bottom of the pan, 5 to 7 minutes.

2. Pour into a mixing bowl and let cool for 15 minutes.

3. Mix in the brown sugar, granulated sugar, eggs, and vanilla. Add the all-purpose flour, baking soda, and salt, followed by the chocolate chips. Stir to combine.

4. Refrigerate the dough for at least 2 hours (and preferably overnight).

5. Preheat the oven to 350°F (175°C). Line a baking sheet with parchment paper.

6. Form the dough into small balls (about 2 tablespoons), then place them on the baking sheet.

7. Bake for 10 to 12 minutes, until the edges of the cookies start to brown.

Christmas Tree Ravioli

PREP TIME 1 HR | COOK TIME 5 MIN | 6 to 8 SERVINGS

My family always had a big Italian-American Christmas when I was a kid: a feast on Christmas Eve with all the relatives, big jugs of wine that my great-grandfather called belly-wash, and more food than we could ever eat. The next day, we'd gather for another meal, and we'd eat leftovers for a week. Now that I'm a parent, I'm learning how to make new holiday traditions for my daughter. One of my favorites is the annual decorating of Christmas cookies, and last year I put my own spin on it: Christmas ravioli. There are no limits here, so fill yourself with some holiday cheer and go wild!

1 batch filling of choice (see chapter 8)

1 batch Spinach Pasta Dough (page 57; see Note below)

¼ batch Turmeric Pasta Dough (page 54)

¼ batch Blue Pasta Dough (page 61)

¼ batch Beet Pasta Dough (page 50)

¼ batch White Pasta Dough (page 64)

Semolina flour, for dusting

1. Fill a piping bag with filling and cut an opening at the tip about ½ inch (1 cm) wide. If you don't have a piping bag, you can use a spoon.

2. Divide the green dough into quarters and work with one piece at a time, leaving the rest covered so it doesn't dry out. Roll out a sheet of dough to the second- or third-thinnest setting on your pasta machine, or about 1 millimeter thick if rolling by hand.

3. Follow the directions for Cookie Cutter Ravioli (page 158), using the green dough and a Christmas tree cookie cutter.

4. Roll the yellow dough to the thinnest setting on your pasta machine, or as thin as possible if rolling by hand.

5. Using a sharp paring knife, an X-Acto knife, or a small cookie cutter, cut stars out of the yellow dough.

6. Press a star on the top of each tree so that it sticks. You may need to brush a small amount of water on the back of the star to help it stick.

7. Use the remaining colors to decorate. Roll out each color to the thinnest setting on your pasta machine, or as thin as you can if rolling by hand.

8. Use the spaghetti attachment on your pasta machine or a knife to cut very thin strips of the white dough, then lay them diagonally across the tree to look like a string of lights. Cut tiny bulbs out of the other colors and place them along the strings. Or cut tiny circles and press them on the trees to look like ornaments. Use your imagination!

9. I recommend cooking these right away. If you leave them in the fridge, even just for a few hours, the filling can seep into the pasta and make it soggy. If you want to make them ahead of time, place the pieces on a floured baking tray or cutting board and freeze them.

10. Cook the ravioli in salted boiling water in batches of 10 to 15, depending on the size of your pot. Cook each batch until tender, 2 to 5 minutes, then use a slotted spoon to carefully remove the ravioli.

NOTE
For a richer hunter green color, make a Classic Pasta Dough (page 38), adding a spoonful of spirulina powder to the eggs.

FRUITS AND VEGETABLES

PREP TIME 60 MIN | COOK TIME 5 MIN | 4 to 6 SERVINGS

We've already incorporated vegetables in the doughs and the sauces, so why not go all the way and make the pasta look like them, too? That's when things can really get trippy: What about a beet dough, shaped like a chili pepper, filled with butternut squash, and served with a tomato sauce? Or keep it simple: Puree some peas to make a dough, shape it into a peapod, use a pea filling, and add a pea sauce. Combine these with some of the flower shapes in this book and you'll truly have a pasta garden on your plate!

Watermelons

1 batch filling of choice (see chapter 8)

1 batch Beet Pasta Dough (page 50)

1 batch Spinach Pasta Dough (page 57)

¼ batch Black Pasta Dough (page 65), optional

1. Fill a piping bag with filling and cut an opening at the tip about ½ inch (1 cm) wide. If you don't have a piping bag, you can use a spoon.

2. Divide each dough into quarters. Work with one piece of each dough at a time while leaving the rest covered. Roll each dough to the second- or third-thinnest setting on your pasta machine, or about 1 millimeter thick if rolling by hand.

3. Use a circular cookie cutter or the top of a glass to cut the green dough into 2½-inch (6.5 cm) circles.

4. Cut the red dough into slightly smaller circles, about 2¼ inches (5.75 cm) in diameter.

5. Place a red circle directly on top of a green circle, positioning it in the center so some of the green is showing all around it (see Tip). Roll each circle with a rolling pin or run it through your pasta machine a couple of times to flatten the layers into one.

6. To make seeded watermelons, cut ¼-inch (6 mm) long teardrop shapes out of the black dough to look like watermelon seeds. Gently press several of them into the red dough (see Tip).

7. Flip the circles over so the red side is facing down and pipe a teaspoon of filling in the middle of each one.

8. Fold the bottom edge of the dough over the filling to the top edge to create a semicircle, fully encapsulating the filling. Press around all the edges to seal the dough, doing your best to remove any air bubbles.

9. Set the watermelon on a floured surface and continue with the rest of the dough.

10. Cook the watermelon in salted, boiling water until tender, 2 to 5 minutes.

TIP

If the dough doesn't stick together, brush on a very small amount of water as glue.

Chili Peppers

1 batch filling of choice (see chapter 8)

1 batch Beet Pasta Dough with Paprika (page 50)

¼ batch Spinach Pasta Dough (page 57)

Semolina flour, for dusting

1. Fill a piping bag with filling and cut an opening at the tip about ½ inch (1 cm) wide. If you don't have a piping bag, you can use a spoon.

2. Divide the red dough into quarters and work with one piece at a time, leaving the rest covered so it doesn't dry out. Run the dough through the widest setting of your pasta machine. Laminate the dough by folding it into thirds and running it through the machine again at the widest setting, and then repeating this process 3 to 4 times (see page 35 for more information).

3. Run the red dough through the machine at the widest setting one last time, or roll the dough into a rectangle about ¼ inch (6 mm) thick.

4. Repeat steps 2 and 3 with the green dough.

5. Cut a strip of green dough about 6 inches (15 cm) long and 1½ inches (4 cm) wide. Cut a rectangle of red dough about 6 inches (15 cm) long and 3½ inches (9 cm) wide.

6. Place the red rectangle and the green strip directly next to each other, so their long edges are touching. Nudge them together so they stick to each other, and roll over them with a rolling pin once or twice to make sure they are secure (see Tip).

7. Trim the top and bottom of the dough to form a neat rectangle. Run the rectangle through your pasta machine, starting on the widest setting, until you reach the second- or third-thinnest setting. If you're rolling by hand, roll the dough until it's about 1 millimeter thick, doing your best to keep a clear line between the red and green doughs.

8. Dust a cutting board with flour, then place the pasta sheet on top. Use a circular cookie cutter or the top of a large cup to cut circles 4 to 5 inches (10 to 13 cm) in diameter. The green should be about 1½ inches (4 cm) at the widest point.

9. Orient the circle so the green strip is on the top. Pipe the filling in the shape of an elongated triangle on the right half of the circle, with the widest part of the triangle on top and overlapping into the green section by about ½ inch (1 cm). The bottom point of the triangle should reach about ½ inch (1 cm) from the bottom edge of the circle.

10. Pick up the right side of the circle and roll it over the filling to make a cone shape. The bottom of the circle should become the point of the cone and the top of the dough should remain open.

11. Press the bottom of the dough into a closed point so no filling can escape.

12. Pinch the dough just above the filling at the top of your shape. There should be some green below the spot you pinched.

FOOD HISTORY

The acidity of the soil, the bright sunlight, and the lack of rain in some parts of Southern Italy are the perfect conditions for growing Calabrian chilis, a hot pepper with a subtle smoky flavor that can be added to pizzas and pastas or turned into an oil and drizzled on just about anything.

TIP

If the doughs aren't sticking together, use your finger to brush a very small amount of water between the edges.

13. Use your fingers to mold the green dough above the pinched spot into the stem of the chili pepper. If it's too long, you can trim it.

14. Set the chili on a floured surface and continue with the rest of the dough.

15. Cook the chilis in salted, boiling water until tender, 2 to 5 minutes.

Carrots

1 batch filling of choice (see chapter 8)

1 batch Roasted Red Pepper Pasta Dough (page 53)

¼ batch Spinach Pasta Dough (page 57)

Semolina flour, for dusting

1. Follow steps 1 through 8 for Chili Peppers, using the orange dough in place of the red dough.

2. Orient the circle so the green strip is on the top. Pipe the filling in the shape of an elongated triangle on the right half of the circle. The widest part of the triangle should be on top but should not overlap with the green dough. The bottom point of the triangle should reach about ½ inch (1 cm) from the bottom edge of the circle.

3. Pinch the dough where the orange and green doughs meet, so the orange carrot is stuffed with filling but the green section is not.

4. Don't pinch the green dough; let it stay loose and open, so it looks like the top of a carrot with the greens cut off.

5. Cook the carrots in salted, boiling water until tender, 2 to 5 minutes.

Peapods

1 batch filling of
  choice (see chapter 8)

1 batch Spinach Pasta
  Dough (page 57)

Semolina flour, for
  dusting

1. Fill a piping bag with filling and cut an opening at the tip about ½ inch (1 cm) wide. If you don't have a piping bag, you can use a spoon.

2. Divide the dough into quarters, working with one quarter at a time and leaving the rest covered. Roll the dough to the second-thinnest or thinnest setting on your pasta machine, or about 1 millimeter thick if rolling by hand.

3. Dust your work surface with flour, then place the pasta sheet horizontally on top. Cut the sheet in half lengthwise to create two long strips of pasta.

4. Pipe three pea-sized balls of filling in a row about 1 inch (2.5 cm) from the bottom edge of the dough, leaving about ¼ inch (6 mm) between them. Then pipe another row of three pea-sized balls about 3 inches (7.5 cm) from the first. Continue piping across the entire pasta sheet.

5. Pick up the bottom edge of the dough and fold it to the top edge, so the filling sits right above the crease. Press down around the filling so it is fully encapsulated and the two layers are sealed. Press down in between the balls of filling so they are clearly defined.

6. Cut the dough into an elongated semicircle around three of the filling balls to make a peapod shape. Repeat with the remaining dough.

7. Use the remaining scraps of dough to cut out a small triangle about the size of the top of your peapod (see Tip 1).

8. Place the triangle on the top of the peapod and pinch the top point so it looks like the stem (see Tip 2).

9. Set the peapod on a floured surface and continue with the rest of the dough.

10. Cook the peapods in salted, boiling water until tender, 2 to 5 minutes.

TIPS

1. Use a fluted pastry roller to cut the bottom edge of the triangle. If you don't have one, cut out tiny triangles along the bottom side to form a jagged edge.

2. If the triangle doesn't stick, brush on a small amount of water.

WITCH HATS AND SANTA HATS

PREP TIME 45 MIN | COOK TIME 5 MIN | 4 to 6 SERVINGS

These hats are inspired by a traditional shape called *cappellacci dei briganti*. That shape was inspired by the wide-brim hats worn by 19th century guerilla fighters known as brigands, who roamed Southern Italy hunting down thieves, looting small towns, and fighting the Italian authorities. They have a complicated legacy and are considered by some to be the forefathers of the Mafia, but in true Italian fashion, they've been memorialized in pasta with this shape. I've adapted it for Halloween and Christmas, but there's really no reason you can't make these little hats all year long.

Witch Hats

1 batch Black Pasta Dough (page 65)

Semolina flour, for dusting

1. Cut the dough into quarters and work with one piece at a time, leaving the rest covered so it doesn't dry out. Roll the dough to the second-thinnest setting on your pasta machine, or about 1 millimeter if rolling by hand.

2. Lightly dust a cutting board with flour. Use a cookie cutter or the top of a wineglass to cut the dough into 2½-inch (6.5 cm) circles.

3. Cover the circles with a bowl or kitchen towel so they don't dry out, and work with one piece at a time.

4. Pick up one circle and wrap it around your index finger to form a cone shape. The dough should overlap slightly and reach a point at the tip of your finger. Press down on the overlapping part so the dough sticks together.

5. Remove your finger and gently bend the bottom of the cone upward to form the brim of the hat.

6. Repeat with the remaining dough.

7. Cook the pasta in salted, boiling water until tender, 3 to 5 minutes.

Santa Hats

1 batch Beet Pasta
Dough with Paprika
(page 50)

½ batch All-00 Vegan
Dough (page 41)

Semolina flour, for
dusting

1. Using the red dough, follow the steps for the Witch Hats (page 177).

2. Take a pea-sized piece of white dough and roll it in your fingers to make a smooth ball.

3. Use your pinky finger to make an indentation in the ball. Then place the ball on top of the hat and press it into place so it sticks. You may need to press firmly, being careful not to smush the hat. You can also add a drop of water to the ball to help it stick.

4. Take a piece of white dough about the size of a marble and use your hands to roll it into a rope. Lay the rope around the edge of the brim of the hat and press it into place so it sticks. You may need to brush the brim with a small amount of water first.

5. Repeat with the remaining hats.

6. Cook the pasta in salted, boiling water until tender, 3 to 5 minutes.

PASTA FACT

Hats are a common
inspiration for pasta
shapes. Two of my favorites
are *cappelletti*, a filled pasta
in the shape of a medieval
hat, and *sombreroni*,
designed to look like
Mexican sombreros.

Mini Lasagnas

PREP TIME 35 MIN | COOK TIME 25 MIN | 2 to 4 SERVINGS

I first started making this dish about fifteen years ago when my (now) husband and I faced a series of lasagna dilemmas: I like mine with a traditional meat sauce, but he's a vegetarian. He prefers his with ricotta, but I like to use mozzarella instead. And, of course, there's the issue of waste. I love lasagna as much as anybody, but after four days of leftovers, I've had enough. Our solution? Individual, totally customizable mini lasagnas. You can swap out whatever vegetables, meats, or cheeses you want. I make these with fresh pasta, but you could certainly use a box of lasagna noodles if you want a quicker version. As an extra touch, make one layer of pasta with a fun pattern to go on top.

½ pound (225 g) ground meat (such as ground beef or Italian sausage)

1 cup (225 g) Weeknight Tomato Sauce (page 192) or jarred tomato sauce

½ batch Classic Pasta Dough (page 38) or 8 boxed lasagna sheets

1 cup shredded fresh mozzarella (120 g) or ricotta (250 g), or a mixture

1 cup (180 g) assorted finely diced vegetables (such as carrots, onions, bell peppers, zucchini, or kale)

¼ cup (15 g) basil, chopped

Salt and pepper

SPECIAL EQUIPMENT
Four 6-ounce (177 ml) ramekins or small bowls

1. Pick your vegetables, cheeses, meats, and herbs.

2. Cook the meat in a skillet over medium-low heat until browned and fully cooked, 5 to 8 minutes. Add the tomato sauce and let simmer until the sauce has reduced slightly, 20 minutes.

3. If you're using fresh pasta, roll the dough to the second- or third-thinnest setting on your pasta machine, or about 1 millimeter thick if rolling by hand. Cut 8 pieces that are each the width of your ramekins and about 1 inch (2.5 cm) long.

4. If you're using boxed lasagna noodles, cook them in salted boiling water until tender enough to fold but not fully cooked, 2 to 3 minutes less than recommended on the box.

5. Preheat the oven to 375°F (190°C). Place a spoonful of sauce in each ramekin.

6. Lay one noodle in the ramekin so the ends of the noodle hang equally over both sides. Add a spoonful of sauce and a spoonful of cheese.

7. Lay another noodle perpendicular to your first noodle to create a cross.

8. Place a small spoonful of sauce in the ramekin, then a thin layer of diced vegetables. Add a thin layer of cheese. Sprinkle on salt, pepper, and basil.

9. Fold in one noodle flap so it rests on your fillings. Add another thin layer of sauce, vegetables, salt, pepper, and basil.

10. Continue folding in flaps and adding layers of your filling until the noodles have all been folded. You may need to press down on the noodles to ensure that the ingredients are spread evenly and everything fits in your ramekin.

11. Top with a final layer of sauce and cheese.

12. Place the ramekins on a baking sheet and bake for about 25 minutes, until the cheese starts to brown and bubble.

7

CHAPTER SEVEN

Sauces

My husband Steve and I first started dating during my senior year of college. I already knew I was moving to New York City after graduation to start law school, and after a few months apart, he moved to join me. With endless takeout options and a lot of reading to do, I hardly ever cooked, and I often got by on the free pizza that student groups would give out to entice people to come to their events.

Steve had been to my family's house for the holidays, so he knew what great cooks they were, and as a vegetarian he was especially partial to my grandmother's eggplant parmigiana. For our first Valentine's Day living together, I asked my mother for the family recipe, including the homemade sauce. Then I got to work, in secret. On Valentine's Day, in between classes, I made a giant batch of eggplant parm and stashed it in our neighbor Shelley's fridge, then rushed home to clean up the evidence before Steve got back from work.

That evening, I told Steve I wasn't really in the mood to do much, since I was so stressed about classes, but I needed him to run out to pick up some paper towels. I had conspired with Shelley for her to cook the eggplant parm at the right time, so as soon as Steve left, I rushed over to get it, then went home to set the table with a new tablecloth and dish set I had bought for the occasion. Then I put on my nicest outfit, lit some candles, and waited for Steve to come home. It's still the nicest Valentine's Day gift I've given him, although to be honest I haven't really done anything since!

I've gone on to cook many different pasta sauces since then, and this chapter includes some of my favorites. There's a pesto that I make in the summer with fresh basil from our garden, a quick broccoli-cheddar sauce I make on weeknights, and many more. Some of these recipes are my takes on Italian-American classics, and others are fun dishes I developed more recently. I enjoy making all of them, and more importantly, my family enjoys eating them. My daughter is especially fond of the Brown Butter with Pecorino and Peas (page 200). Unless otherwise noted, each recipe is designed for one batch of homemade pasta or a 1-pound (454 g) box of dried pasta.

Brown Butter with Toasted Hazelnuts and Sage

PREP TIME 5 MIN | COOK TIME 10 MIN | 4 to 6 SERVINGS

If you haven't experienced the wonders of brown butter, it's past time you tried it. It starts as plain old butter, but then it's cooked on a stovetop until the milk solids are toasty brown, transforming this simple ingredient into something magical. It has a bold, slightly nutty taste that will instantly bring your food to the next level. Use it to make the most amazing chocolate chip cookies (page 166), or pour it over pasta for an easy, tasty sauce. It's very rich (after all, it's just butter) so you don't need a lot of it, and it's light in color, so it won't cover up the beautiful pasta you've made!

Salt, for the pasta water

1 pound (454 g) pasta of choice

1 cup (225 g) unsalted butter, sliced into 1-inch (2.5 cm) pieces

⅓ cup (45 g) hazelnuts, roughly chopped

10 to 15 small sage leaves

¼ cup (30 g) grated Parmesan

1. Bring a pot of salted water to a boil and cook your pasta according to recipe or package directions. Drain the pasta and plate.

2. While the water is coming to a boil, make the sauce.

3. Place the butter and hazelnuts in a wide, light-colored saucepan over medium heat (see Tip 1). Let cook until the butter melts completely and starts to bubble, 3 to 4 minutes, then sizzle and foam, another 2 minutes. Stir or swirl the pan to prevent burning.

4. When the foaming calms down slightly and the noise gets a little quieter, 1 more minute, add the sage leaves.

5. Stir and watch closely because the butter can go from perfect to burned very quickly. After another minute, the butter will start to turn golden-brown and smell nutty, and you'll notice lots of small brown specks—toasted milk solids—on the bottom of the pan (see Tip 2). Remove the pan from the heat.

6. Use a large spoon to drizzle the sauce directly over your pasta. Or, if you prefer, you can add your pasta to the saucepan and swirl it around to distribute the sauce.

7. Sprinkle with Parmesan and serve.

PAIRS WELL WITH: *Sacchetti* (page 118), *Mezzelune* (page 121), *Ravioli* (page 122), *Ravioli Al'Uovo* (page 130), *Caramelle* (page 134), *Sunflowers* (page 144), *Succulent Ravioli* (page 161), or any filled pasta.

TIPS

1. Avoid using a pan with a dark or black surface, because it will be difficult to see the color changes in the butter.
2. Cook the butter long enough for these milk solids to appear, but not so long that they burn and turn black.

FOOD HISTORY

In the United States, we often think of olive oil as an Italian staple. This is due to the large influx of Italian immigrants from Southern Italy, where olive oil was predominant. In Northern Italy, butter was traditionally used as a fat source instead.

Burst Cherry Tomato Sauce

PREP TIME 5 MIN | COOK TIME 45 MIN | 4 to 6 SERVINGS

When I moved to New York City to attend law school, we rented a little one-bedroom apartment in a dilapidated, rent-stabilized building on the Upper West Side. The kitchen was minuscule and the oven only worked about half the time—more than once I had to rush over to my neighbors' apartment in the middle of dinner to finish cooking. But I loved that apartment because it had something rare in NYC: a giant, private rooftop terrace, the perfect spot for growing flowers, vegetables, fruits, and herbs. We'd end up with so many bowls of sweet, juicy tomatoes that I never knew what to do with them; I wish I had developed this recipe back then! Cherry tomatoes are the true stars of this dish, roasted to perfection with garlic and thyme and then topped off with some basil and grated cheese. The ingredients are simple, but the taste is amazing.

½ cup (120 ml) olive oil

2 pints cherry tomatoes (about 1¼ pounds/570 g)

10 garlic cloves

4 to 5 thyme sprigs

1 teaspoon salt, divided, plus more for the pasta water

1 pound (454 g) pasta of choice

1 small palmful (about ¼ cup/15 g) basil leaves, julienned

½ cup (60 g) grated Parmesan, plus more to taste

1. Preheat the oven to 350°F (175°C).

2. Pour the oil into a 9 × 13-inch (23 × 33 cm) baking dish. Add the tomatoes, garlic, and thyme, then sprinkle with ½ teaspoon salt. Stir everything together to coat the tomatoes in oil.

3. Bake for about 45 minutes, until the tomatoes start to burst and look roasted but have not shriveled up.

4. Meanwhile, bring a pot of salted water to a boil and cook your pasta according to recipe or package directions.

5. Remove the baking dish from the oven and take out the thyme sprigs. Mash the garlic cloves with a fork (see Note).

6. Add the basil, Parmesan, and the remaining ½ teaspoon salt to the tomatoes and stir. Add the cooked pasta and mix to coat with the sauce.

7. Serve with additional Parmesan sprinkled on top, if desired.

PAIRS WELL WITH: *Tagliatelle* (page 102), *Farfalle* (page 107), *Garganelli* (page 108), *Caramelle* (page 134), *Long Farfalle* (page 143), *Candy* (page 148), *Pinwheels* (page 151), *Witch Hats and Santa Hats* (page 177).

NOTE

For a smoother sauce, you can also mash the tomatoes, but I prefer to leave them intact for a chunkier texture.

FOOD HISTORY

Humans have been collecting olives since at least 8000 BCE and turning them into olive oil since before 4000 BCE. Throughout history, olive oil has been used in cooking, religious ceremonies, soap making, cosmetics, and as fuel for lamps. It's considered one of the staples of the Mediterranean diet, and Italy is the world's second-largest producer of olive oil after Spain.

Garlic Cream Sauce with Pancetta and Crispy Shallots

PREP TIME 10 MIN | COOK TIME 25 MIN | 4 to 6 SERVINGS

This sauce comes together very quickly but packs a cheesy, garlicky punch. If you leave out the pancetta and shallots, you can make this in the time it takes to cook your pasta, but I like adding them for some extra richness and crunch. You can swap out the pancetta for another protein, and if you're a garlic lover, you can add a few extra cloves.

3 shallots

½ cup (120 ml) vegetable oil

4 ounces (110 g) pancetta (or bacon, if you can't find pancetta)

1 pound (454 g) pasta of choice

4 tablespoons unsalted butter

4 to 5 garlic cloves, crushed or minced

1 teaspoon salt, plus more for the pasta water

½ teaspoon black pepper

¾ cup (180 ml) heavy cream

½ cup (60 g) grated Parmesan

2 tablespoons chopped parsley

1. Peel and cut the shallots into ⅛-inch (3 mm) slices. Use a mandoline, if you have one, to make the slices as even as possible.

2. Place the shallots in a large frying pan and add the oil just to cover. Turn the heat to high and cook until the oil is bubbly, 3 to 4 minutes. Reduce the heat to medium-low and cook until the shallots start to brown, stirring occasionally, 7 to 10 minutes.

3. Remove the shallots with a slotted spoon and transfer to a paper towel to drain. The shallots will continue to cook after you remove them from the heat, so don't wait to take them out of the pan until they're fully brown or they will burn. Rinse the pan to remove the shallot flavor.

4. Slice the pancetta into ½-inch (1 cm) pieces and place them in the pan with enough room that they're not touching.

5. Turn the heat to medium and cook, stirring occasionally, until the fat renders off and the pancetta turns brown, 5 to 7 minutes. Remove the pancetta and set aside. Drain the fat.

6. Bring a pot of salted water to a boil. Cook your pasta according to recipe or package directions.

7. While the pasta is cooking, slice the butter into 1-inch (2.5 cm) pieces and add them to the frying pan over medium heat.

8. Add the garlic and cook until just starting to brown, about 1 minute. Reduce the heat to medium-low. Add the salt and pepper, then slowly pour in the cream, whisking constantly.

9. When the sauce has come together and thickened, in 4 to 6 minutes, turn off the heat and gradually stir in the Parmesan and parsley. Taste and add more salt and pepper if desired.

10. Add the sauce to the pasta and top with the pancetta and shallots.

PAIRS WELL WITH: *Barchette* (page 99), *Tagliatelle* (page 102), *Fusi Istriani* (page 111), *Funghetti* (page 114), *Long Farfalle* (page 143), *Candy* (page 148), *Pinwheels* (page 151), *Witch Hats and Santa Hats* (page 177).

Fast Bolognese Sauce

PREP TIME 10 MIN | COOK TIME 65 MIN | 4 to 6 SERVINGS

Bolognese sauce is a classic Italian dish that has deep, hearty flavors developed from hours of slowly cooking the ingredients over low heat. If you're short on time, it can be difficult to mimic this rich flavor, but sometimes you're craving a good Bolognese and don't have four hours to spare! This speedy version comes together in just over an hour; it's a thick, meaty tomato sauce that just might satisfy your Bolognese cravings perfectly.

1 small yellow onion

1 carrot

2 celery stalks

2 garlic cloves

2 tablespoons olive oil

1 pound (454 g) ground beef (80 to 85 percent lean)

1 teaspoon salt, plus more for the pasta water

½ teaspoon black pepper

One 28-ounce (794 g) can whole San Marzano tomatoes

2 tablespoons tomato paste

¼ cup (60 ml) milk

1 pound (454 g) pasta of choice

¼ cup (15 g) chopped basil

¼ cup (30 g) grated Parmesan, optional

1. Use a knife or a food processor to finely chop the onion, carrot, celery, and garlic as small as you can (see Note).

2. In a wide skillet or saucepan, heat the oil over medium heat, then add the vegetable mixture. Cook until the vegetables become paler in color, 8 to 10 minutes. If they start to burn on the bottom of the pan, lower the heat or add a little more oil.

3. Add the beef, breaking it up with a spatula, and sprinkle with salt and pepper. Cook until there are no more pink spots, about 10 minutes.

4. Crush the tomatoes with your hands or puree them in a blender. Add them to the pan along with the tomato paste. Add milk, then stir everything together.

5. Reduce the heat to medium-low and let simmer for 40 minutes, stirring and tasting occasionally and adding salt if necessary, until the tomatoes have reduced significantly and most of the liquid has evaporated. If the sauce starts to dry up completely and looks like it may burn, lower the heat.

6. Meanwhile, bring a pot of salted water to a boil and cook your pasta according to recipe or package directions.

7. Add the basil to the sauce and let cook until it is incorporated into the sauce, 5 minutes.

8. Add the cooked pasta to the sauce and serve with Parmesan sprinkled on top if desired.

PAIRS WELL WITH: *Barchette* (page 99), *Tagliatelle* (page 102), *Garganelli* (page 108), *Fusi Istriani* (page 111), *Funghetti* (page 114), *Four-Petal Flowers* (page 140), *Candy* (page 148), *Pinwheels* (page 151), *Witch Hats and Santa Hats* (page 177).

NOTE

The goal is for the vegetables to "disappear" into the sauce, so they're imparting flavor but you don't see any large pieces.

FOOD HISTORY

The combination of cooked onion, celery, carrots, and sometimes garlic is called a *soffritto*, and it forms the base of many Italian sauces, soups, stews, and risottos. To maximize the flavor of each ingredient, a *soffritto* is often made by sautéing the onions first, then adding the garlic, and finally the carrots and celery, and it's an easy way to add rich flavor to a dish.

Weeknight Tomato Sauce

PREP TIME 10 MIN | COOK TIME 45 MIN | 4 to 6 SERVINGS

When I was growing up, we called this recipe "Quick Sauce." It wasn't the deep, rich tomato sauce that simmered all day on the stove on Sundays (see Sunday Sauce, page 204), but it was the dish my mom whipped up on a Wednesday night when we were craving pasta and the sauce reserves in the freezer had been depleted. This sauce is all about the tomatoes you use, so be sure to pick good ones. Look for cans of whole San Marzano tomatoes: sweet, plum-shaped tomatoes from Italy. If you want to splurge, buy cans with the "DOP" emblem, which means the tomatoes were grown in the San Marzano region of Italy. They're rather pricey, though, so I often buy less expensive varieties grown in the U.S.; just look for something with "Italian Style" or "San Marzano Style" on the label. This recipe uses whole tomatoes that produce a really thick, rustic sauce, but if you prefer something smoother, you can blend all the ingredients together before simmering.

2 tablespoons olive oil

1 to 2 garlic cloves, thinly sliced

One 28-ounce (794 g) can whole San Marzano or San Marzano–style tomatoes

½ teaspoon salt, plus more for the pasta water

½ teaspoon red pepper flakes, optional

1 small palmful basil (about ¼ cup/15 g), finely chopped

1 pound (454 g) pasta of choice

¼ cup (30 g) grated Parmesan, optional

1. Heat the oil in a wide saucepan or skillet over medium heat (see Tip).

2. Add the garlic and cook until it just starts to brown, stirring occasionally, for 1 to 2 minutes, being careful not to let it burn.

3. Add the can of tomatoes, including the liquid, and the salt and stir everything together. If you want a little heat, add the red pepper flakes.

4. Lower the heat to medium-low and let simmer until you can crush the tomatoes easily with a fork, about 15 minutes.

5. Crush the tomatoes, mix them together, and taste the sauce. Add more salt if necessary.

6. Cook for 15 more minutes, stirring occasionally, then add the basil.

7. Let simmer for 10 more minutes while you cook your pasta in salted, boiling water. If the sauce has started to dry out while the pasta is cooking, add a spoonful of pasta water along with the pasta. Combine the sauce and pasta in a large bowl and serve with Parmesan sprinkled on top if desired.

PAIRS WELL WITH: All.

TIP
The wider the pan, the better, because it will allow the sauce to cook more quickly.

FOOD HISTORY
Although tomatoes are practically synonymous with Italian cooking today, they didn't arrive in Italy until the 1500s after Spain colonized the Americas and learned about the plant from the Aztecs.

Pesto with Green Beans and Potatoes

PREP TIME 15 MIN | COOK TIME 20 MIN | 4 to 6 SERVINGS

As an adult I've moved around a bit—from New York to California to North Carolina and back to New York again—but I've always made sure to have a little outdoor space, and I've always grown basil. Basil grows quite abundantly, and one plant is enough to supply a summer's worth of leaves. Pesto is the quintessential basil dish—it's bright and flavorful and should be eaten all summer long. In Liguria, where basil pesto originates, it's traditionally served with green beans and potatoes.

3 small Yukon Gold potatoes (about ½ pound/227 g)

2 cups (about 100 g) loosely packed basil leaves

1 to 2 garlic cloves, unpeeled

2 tablespoons pine nuts

1 tablespoon lemon juice, plus more to taste

½ teaspoon salt, plus more for the pasta water

½ cup (120 ml) olive oil

2½ tablespoons grated Parmesan, plus more for serving

1½ tablespoons grated Pecorino Romano

¾ pound (340 g) green beans, trimmed and cut into 1-inch (2.5 cm) pieces

1 pound (454 g) pasta of choice

3 tablespoons unsalted butter, sliced

1. Cut the potatoes into ¼-inch (6 mm) slices, then cut the slices in half.

2. Optionally, to give your pesto a bright green color, blanch the basil. Bring a pot of water to a boil. Add the basil for about 10 seconds, then immediately transfer to a bowl filled with ice water. Let cool, then drain and set aside.

3. Heat a sauté pan over medium heat, then add the garlic. When the skins start to brown, after 2 to 3 minutes, lower the heat and add the pine nuts.

4. Cook until the pine nuts are toasty brown, another 1 to 2 minutes, stirring frequently so they cook evenly. Watch closely, because they burn easily. Remove the pine nuts and garlic from the heat and let cool. When the garlic is cool enough to touch, remove the skins.

5. Wring out any excess water from the basil, then place the basil, garlic, pine nuts, lemon juice, and salt in a food processor. Pulse in 5-to-10-second bursts until the ingredients have been chopped evenly.

6. With the food processor running, slowly add the oil until the pesto looks creamy and smooth but not watery. (You might not need to use all the oil.)

7. Add in the Parmesan and Pecorino and pulse very briefly, just until incorporated. Taste, then add more salt or lemon juice if necessary.

8. Bring a large pot of salted water to a boil and add the potatoes. After about 5 minutes, add the green beans. After another 5 minutes, add the pasta. Cook according to recipe or package directions.

9. While the pasta is cooking, place a large spoonful of pesto into a serving bowl. Add 2 tablespoons of pasta water and the butter and stir together.

10. When the pasta and vegetables are done cooking, drain and add them to the bowl. Stir in the rest of the pesto.

11. Serve with additional grated Parmesan if desired.

PAIRS WELL WITH: *Barchette* (page 99), *Tagliatelle* (page 102), *Farfalle* (page 107), *Fusi Istriani* (page 111), *Funghetti* (page 114), *Cavatelli* (page 117), *Four-Petal Flowers* (page 140), *Candy* (page 148), *Pinwheels* (page 151).

Cauliflower-Garlic Sauce

PREP TIME 5 MIN | COOK TIME 20 MIN | 4 to 6 SERVINGS

When I make fresh pasta with my family, this is the sauce we use most often. It's simple, comes together quickly, and tastes great, which is exactly what you're looking for after all that kneading and rolling. This sauce uses a big spoonful of pasta water, the starchy, salty water that develops after the pasta cooks in it. Pasta water adds a richness to any sauce, helping to thicken it; it's also a key player in getting the sauce to adhere to the noodles.

2 tablespoons olive oil

1 medium yellow onion, diced

2 garlic cloves, thinly sliced

1 teaspoon salt, plus more for the pasta water

½ teaspoon red pepper flakes

1 large cauliflower, cut into small florets

1 pound (454 g) pasta of choice

½ cup (60 g) grated Parmesan, plus more for serving

1. Bring a pot of salted water to a boil.

2. Heat the oil in a large skillet over medium heat, then add the onion. Cook, stirring occasionally, until translucent, 8 minutes.

3. Add the garlic, salt, and red pepper flakes and cook until the garlic just starts to brown, about 1 minute.

4. Stir in the cauliflower. Cover the pan and cook until the cauliflower is soft and tender, about 10 minutes, stirring occasionally.

5. When the water is boiling, add the pasta. Cook according to recipe or package directions, then drain, reserving some of the pasta water.

6. Add ¼ cup (60 ml) pasta water to the cauliflower and stir. Add the cooked pasta to the pan. Add the Parmesan, then mix everything together until the cheese melts (see Tip).

7. Serve with additional Parmesan sprinkled on top if desired.

PAIRS WELL WITH: *Tagliatelle* (page 102), *Farfalle* (page 107), *Garganelli* (page 108), *Funghetti* (page 114), *Long Farfalle* (page 143), *Candy* (page 148).

TIP
If you're having trouble mixing everything in the pan, transfer to a large bowl.

FOOD FACT
This recipe is a twist on a classic Italian dish, *spaghetti aglio e olio*. With just two ingredients as its base—olive oil and garlic—it's a popular recipe for young Italians to make when arriving home after a long weekend night.

Creamy Butternut Squash Sauce with Roasted Shallots and Garlic

PREP TIME 15 MIN | COOK TIME 50 MIN | 4 to 6 SERVINGS

The first job I ever had was at a cider donut counter at an apple orchard, when I was in high school. In the fall, people would come in droves to drink apple cider and pick their own pumpkins. I can't say I loved it at the time, but looking back I realize it gave me a certain affinity for that time of year, when the weather cools down, the trees turn fiery red, and there are pumpkins everywhere. That's what this dish reminds me of: strolling outside on chilly November days, leaves crunching under your feet, when all you want is a hearty bowl of something warm to come home to.

1 medium butternut squash

2 shallots, peeled and halved vertically

Olive oil

Salt

Black pepper

1 head of garlic

1 pound (454 g) pasta of choice

Pinch of ground nutmeg

1 cup (240 ml) heavy cream

1. Preheat the oven to 400°F (200°C). Line a baking sheet with parchment paper.

2. Slice the squash in half vertically (see Tip). Scoop out the seeds, then place both squash halves, cut side up, on the baking sheet. Add the shallots to the baking sheet.

3. Drizzle the squash and shallots with oil, then rub the oil into the squash to cover the entire surface. Sprinkle with ½ teaspoon salt and a pinch of pepper.

4. Slice off the top of the head of garlic, about ½ inch (1 cm) from the end, to expose all the cloves. Drizzle with oil, then sprinkle with a pinch of salt and pepper. Wrap the garlic in aluminum foil and place it on the baking sheet.

5. Cook the vegetables for 35 to 40 minutes, until the squash is tender enough to pierce easily with a fork. Remove and let cool.

6. Meanwhile, bring a pot of salted water to a boil. Cook your pasta according to recipe or package directions. Drain and set aside.

7. Scoop the flesh of the squash into a food processor. Add the shallots and garlic cloves (squeeze the garlic head to remove them).

8. Add the nutmeg, then puree the vegetables until smooth. Taste and add more salt and pepper if necessary.

9. Pour the puree into a saucepan, then add the heavy cream. Heat on medium-low until the sauce has thickened, about 10 minutes, and then add to the pasta.

PAIRS WELL WITH: *Tagliatelle* (page 102), *Farfalle* (page 107), *Garganelli* (page 108), *Fusi Istriani* (page 111), *Rose Ravioli* (page 155), *Succulent Ravioli* (page 161), *Witch Hats and Santa Hats* (page 177).

TIP

If the squash is difficult to cut, pierce it with a knife several times, then microwave it for 3 to 4 minutes. This should soften the skin enough to make it easier to cut.

Brown Butter with Pecorino and Peas

PREP TIME 10 MIN | COOK TIME 45 MIN | 4 to 6 SERVINGS

One of my ultimate pasta comfort dishes is about as simple as they come. After I cook and drain my pasta, and while it's still hot, I add some slices of butter and a handful of grated cheese. I mix it all together so the butter and cheese melt, and then (sometimes) throw in some veggies, herbs, spices, or whatever else I have on hand. It's what I eat when I don't feel like cooking or just want something I know I'll like. This is a slightly more elevated version, using brown butter and a lot of pepper, but it retains the heart of the original.

1 stick (113 g) unsalted butter, sliced into 1-inch (2.5 cm pieces)

1 pound (454 g) pasta of choice

Salt, for the pasta water

1 cup (140 g) peas, fresh or frozen

1 cup (120 g) grated Pecorino, plus more for serving

1½ teaspoons black pepper

1. Place the butter in a wide saucepan over medium heat (see Tip 1). Let cook until the butter starts to bubble, 3 to 4 minutes, then cook until the butter starts to sizzle and foam, another 2 minutes. Stir or swirl the pan to prevent burning.

2. Stir and watch closely, because the butter can go from perfect to burned very quickly. After 2 minutes, the butter will start to turn golden-brown and smell nutty, and you'll notice lots of small brown specks—toasted milk solids—on the bottom of the pan (see Tip 2). Remove the pan from the heat, then pour the butter into a heat-safe dish (see Tip 3).

3. Place the butter in the refrigerator to solidify, 30 to 40 minutes (see Tip 4). Give it a good stir so the brown bits that have settled on the bottom are well mixed.

4. Bring a pot of salted water to a boil, then add the pasta and peas. Cook the pasta according to recipe or package directions. About a minute before the pasta is done, remove ¼ cup (60 ml) pasta water. Drain the pasta and return it to the pot off the heat.

5. Add the butter, Pecorino, and pepper, along with a spoonful of pasta water, to the pasta and stir together. The heat of the pasta should melt the butter and cheese and form a sauce.

6. Serve with additional Pecorino sprinkled on top if desired.

PAIRS WELL WITH: *Barchette* (page 99), *Farfalle* (page 107), *Garganelli* (page 108), *Funghetti* (page 114), *Cavatelli* (page 117), *Witch Hats and Santa Hats* (page 177).

TIPS

1. Avoid using a pan with a dark or black surface because it will be difficult to see the color changes in the butter.

2. Cook the butter long enough for these milk solids to appear, but not so long that they burn and turn black.

3. After you make the brown butter, you can mix in garlic, fresh herbs, cinnamon, or other ingredients before it solidifies. Once it's solid, you can also spread it on toast, waffles, or crackers.

4. You can skip this step and make the sauce right away, but I find the butter combines better with the other ingredients when it is somewhat solid.

Pink Sauce

PREP TIME 5 MIN | COOK TIME 45 MIN | 4 to 6 SERVINGS

Before you dive into this recipe, let's get one thing out of the way: This sauce isn't actually pink. The final color is more of a dull orange, but the sauce gets its name from the fact that we're combining a red (tomato sauce) with a white (cream) that, in theory, would yield pink. I've seen similar dishes called a "blush" or "rose" sauce, so I know I'm not alone in my thinking here. It's a bit like a vodka sauce without the vodka, but with the addition of mozzarella at the end to make it extra cheesy. For a quick dinner, skip the homemade tomato sauce and use a jar instead—you'll be able to whip this up in 15 minutes!

One 28-ounce (794 g) can whole San Marzano tomatoes

1 small palmful (about ¼ cup/15 g) basil leaves

2 tablespoons olive oil

1 garlic clove

1 teaspoon salt, plus more for the pasta water

1 cup (240 ml) heavy cream

½ cup (60 g) grated Parmesan, plus more for serving

½ teaspoon red pepper flakes, optional

1 pound (454 g) pasta of choice

1½ cups (175 g) shredded fresh mozzarella

1. Puree the tomatoes, basil, olive oil, garlic, and salt in a blender until smooth.

2. Pour the tomato mixture into a wide saucepan over medium heat. Bring to a boil, then reduce the heat to medium-low and let simmer for about 30 minutes, until the mixture is reduced to a thick sauce.

3. Taste and add more salt if necessary. Stir in the cream, Parmesan, and red pepper flakes, if using. Cook until the Parmesan has melted completely and the sauce is smooth, 10 more minutes.

4. Meanwhile, bring a pot of salted water to a boil. Cook your pasta according to recipe or package directions.

5. Drain the pasta and add it to the saucepan. Mix to coat the pasta in the sauce.

6. Stir in the mozzarella until it starts to melt. It won't melt completely but rather will be stringy, leading to a dish that's gooey and cheesy! Top with grated Parmesan if desired.

PAIRS WELL WITH: *Barchette* (page 99), *Farfalle* (page 107), *Garganelli* (page 108), *Funghetti* (page 114), *Cavatelli* (page 117), *Four-Petal Flowers* (page 140), *Witch Hats and Santa Hats* (page 177).

FOOD HISTORY

Penne alla vodka likely originated around the 1970s, but it's not clear where it first started. A New York chef claims to have invented it, but several Italian sources insist it was already well-known in Italy before Americans "discovered" it.

Sunday Sauce

PREP TIME 10 MIN | COOK TIME 3½ HRS | 8 to 12 SERVINGS

Some Italian Americans call the big pot of tomatoes and meat stewing on the stove every weekend the "Sunday Gravy," but in my family we just call it Sauce. It was always simmering in the kitchen every Sunday, then served throughout the week as leftovers. It's comfort in a dish, the food that reminds me of home more than any other. Now, if you ask 100 Italian Americans how to make a Sunday Sauce, you'll probably get 110 different answers, and I don't believe there's a "right" way to make it. You can use different meats and vegetables, include tomato paste or wine or leave them out. At the end of the day, all that matters is that it tastes good!

1½ pounds (680 g) boneless pork ribs

2 teaspoons salt, divided, plus more for the pasta water

¼ teaspoon black pepper

¼ cup (60 ml) olive oil, divided

Four 28-ounce (794 g) cans whole San Marzano tomatoes

8 garlic cloves

1 cup (60 g) basil leaves

1 pound (454 g) sweet Italian sausage links

¼ cup (60 ml) red wine

2 pounds (908 g) pasta of choice

1. Season the ribs on both sides with ½ teaspoon salt and pepper.

2. Heat 2 tablespoons oil in a large pot over medium heat. Add the pork ribs and cook until both sides are browned, about 10 minutes, flipping halfway through. Remove the ribs and set aside on a large plate.

3. While the ribs are cooking, add one can of tomatoes, the garlic, and basil to a blender and puree. Leave in the blender while you finish cooking the meats.

4. Return the empty pot to the heat. If the pot has dried out, add more oil, then add the sausage and cook until browned, about 5 minutes. Transfer to the plate with the ribs.

5. Deglaze the pot by adding the wine and scraping all the brown bits off the bottom until the wine has evaporated, about 3 minutes.

6. Pour the blended tomatoes into the pot and stir. Return the meat to the pot.

7. Blend the remaining three cans of tomatoes and add to the pot. Stir in 1 teaspoon salt and 2 tablespoons olive oil and bring to a boil, about 5 minutes.

8. Lower the heat and let the sauce simmer, stirring occasionally, until it has reduced considerably, darkened in color, and developed a deep, rich flavor, about 3 hours, tasting occasionally and adding more salt if necessary (see Tip). Halfway through cooking, cut the sausages in half, to add more flavor.

9. Bring a large pot of salted water to a boil, then cook the pasta according to recipe or package directions. Drain, then combine with sauce in a large bowl.

PAIRS WELL WITH: All.

TIP

Don't be shy about adding salt, because it will really bring out the flavor of the tomatoes.

FOOD HISTORY

Much of the Italian-American cuisine we know today is thanks to the arrival of immigrants from Southern Italy in the late 1800s. Cheap meat was more plentiful in American cities than it had been in Italy, resulting in more meat-heavy classics like Spaghetti and Meatballs and Chicken Parmigiana.

Red Pesto

PREP TIME 10 MIN | COOK TIME 15 MIN | 4 to 6 SERVINGS

When you hear the word "pesto," you likely think of a green basil sauce like the one on page 195. That's technically a *pesto alla Genovese*, which comes from the northern Italian city of Genoa. But Sicily has its own pesto: *pesto rosso*, a beautiful spread made with sun-dried tomatoes. You can put it on a sandwich, spread it on grilled chicken, or even add some to mashed potatoes or scrambled eggs. This recipe incorporates some pasta water to make the pesto a bit saucier, but feel free to use it in its original form.

1 pound (454 g) pasta of choice

One 8-ounce (227 g) jar of sun-dried tomatoes (packed in oil)

½ cup (60 g) grated Parmesan, plus more for serving

⅓ cup (50 g) dry-roasted almonds

¼ cup (15 g) basil leaves

2 garlic cloves

½ teaspoon salt, plus more for the pasta water

Pinch of red pepper flakes, optional

¼ cup (60 ml) olive oil

1. Bring a pot of salted water to a boil, then cook your pasta according to recipe or package directions. Drain and set aside.

2. Meanwhile, place the sun-dried tomatoes (and the oil from the jar), Parmesan, almonds, basil, garlic, salt, and red pepper flakes, if using, in a food processor. Blend until the ingredients are finely chopped and start to form a thick paste.

3. With the food processor running, slowly stream in the olive oil to form a creamy paste.

4. Transfer the pesto to a saucepan and turn the heat to low while the pasta cooks.

5. When the pasta is done, drain, reserving ¼ cup (60 ml) of pasta water. Add the pasta water to the pesto, then combine with the pasta in a large bowl.

6. Serve with additional Parmesan sprinkled on top if desired.

PAIRS WELL WITH: *Fusi Istriani* (page 111), *Funghetti* (page 114), *Cestini* (page 129), *Long Farfalle* (page 143), *Candy* (page 148), *Cookie Cutter Ravioli* (page 158), *Succulent Ravioli* (page 161).

FOOD HISTORY

Italians traditionally dried tomatoes on their ceramic rooftops to bring out their sweet flavor and then preserved them in olive oil. This allowed them to eat tomatoes all year long.

Broccoli-Cheddar Sauce

PREP TIME 10 MIN | COOK TIME 15 MIN | 4 to 6 SERVINGS

Broccoli-cheddar soup is a well-loved dish, so why not take that flavor combination and turn it into a pasta sauce? This sauce is very quick to make, but it's cheesy, creamy, and full of flavor. Use a sharp or extra-sharp cheddar, and don't buy pre-shredded cheese, because it won't melt as well. Feel free to swap out the milk for half-and-half or cream if you want an even richer version, or use cauliflower instead of broccoli. I like to serve mine with hot sauce drizzled on top for some extra spice or with a few crunchy toppings on top. Bacon, breadcrumbs, crispy onions, or pancetta would all be great!

1 pound (454 g) pasta of choice

1 large head of broccoli, cut into florets (about 4 cups/360 g)

2 tablespoons unsalted butter

1 garlic clove, crushed or minced

2 tablespoons all-purpose flour

1½ cups (360 ml) milk

1 teaspoon Dijon mustard

1 teaspoon salt

½ teaspoon black pepper

14 ounces (400 g) sharp cheddar, shredded

1. Bring a pot of salted water to a boil. Add the pasta and the broccoli and cook for about 5 minutes (see Tip).

2. Meanwhile, melt the butter in a wide saucepan over medium heat, then add the garlic.

3. After a minute, whisk in the flour.

4. Slowly add in the milk, whisking vigorously. Continue stirring until the sauce thickens, 3 to 4 minutes. Stir in the mustard, salt, and pepper.

5. Lower the heat, then add the cheese, one handful at a time, stirring after each addition until it's completely melted, to form a smooth, thick sauce.

6. Drain the pasta and broccoli and add to the sauce. Stir to combine.

PAIRS WELL WITH: *Barchette* (page 99), *Garganelli* (page 108), *Funghetti* (page 114), *Cavatelli* (page 117), *Candy* (page 148), *Witch Hats and Santa Hats* (page 177).

TIP

If you're using a box of dry pasta, cook the pasta for about 10 minutes (according to the box's instructions) and add the broccoli about 5 minutes after adding the pasta.

Lemon-Ricotta Sauce with Roasted Asparagus and Toasted Breadcrumbs

PREP TIME 10 MIN | COOK TIME 25 MIN | 4 to 6 SERVINGS

Italian cooking is not always very complicated, and it often focuses on simple, fresh ingredients cooked to perfection to bring out their natural flavor. With high-quality ingredients and vegetables picked when they're at their tastiest, you don't need much else. That's what this sauce embodies: The ingredients are simple, but they balance each other nicely and each one shines through. Ricotta plays a starring role in this dish, and if you have time, it's worth it to make some from scratch (see page 220), but I certainly won't fault you for using store-bought!

2 tablespoons salted butter

1 cup (110 g) Panko-style breadcrumbs

1 garlic clove, crushed

1 bunch asparagus (about 1 pound/454 g)

2 tablespoons olive oil

1 teaspoon salt, plus more for the pasta water

½ teaspoon black pepper, plus more to taste

½ teaspoon red pepper flakes, optional

1 pound (454 g) pasta of choice

1½ cups (400 g) ricotta (see page 220)

1 cup (120 g) grated Pecorino Romano

3 tablespoons lemon juice

1 tablespoon lemon zest

1. Preheat the oven to 425°F (220°C).

2. Melt the butter in a large skillet over medium heat. Add the breadcrumbs and garlic and stir to coat evenly in butter. Toast for 4 to 5 minutes, stirring frequently so they don't burn, then remove from the heat and set aside.

3. Break off the bottom ends of the asparagus and discard. Cut the asparagus into 1½-inch (4 cm) pieces and place them in a large bowl with the oil, salt, black pepper, and red pepper flakes, if using. Mix to coat the asparagus.

4. Lay the asparagus on a baking sheet and cook for 10 to 15 minutes, until the widest part is tender enough to easily pierce with a fork.

5. Meanwhile, bring a large pot of water to a boil. Cook the pasta according to recipe or package directions.

6. While the pasta is cooking, add the ricotta, Pecorino, lemon juice, a sprinkle of salt, and a sprinkle of pepper to the skillet and heat over medium-low.

7. When the pasta is done, reserve a cup of pasta water, then drain the pasta and transfer to a large bowl. Stir a spoonful of pasta water into the sauce to form a creamy consistency. Add the sauce and the asparagus to the pasta and mix.

8. Serve with breadcrumbs and lemon zest sprinkled on top.

PAIRS WELL WITH: *Barchette* (page 99), *Farfalle* (page 107), *Fusi Istriani* (page 111), *Funghetti* (page 114), *Tortellini* (page 125), *Long Farfalle* (page 143), *Candy* (page 148).

FOOD FACT

Ricotta is an incredibly versatile ingredient in Italian cooking, used in both savory and sweet dishes. You can find it in everything from lasagna to cannoli to meatballs.

Mint-Pea Sauce with Radishes and Parmesan

PREP TIME 10 MIN | COOK TIME 20 MIN | 4 to 6 SERVINGS

I have to give my husband Steve credit for this sauce, since he often makes a thicker version of it to spread on toast. It's bright, fresh, and incredibly versatile: It can be used on sandwiches, as a veggie dip, or even just eaten on its own. I've added a few ingredients to turn this into a pasta sauce, but even so this comes together quickly and can be made in the time it takes to cook your pasta. And don't be afraid to use frozen peas! If you're anything like me, you probably already have a bag of them stuffed somewhere at the bottom of your freezer.

3 red radishes, trimmed

13 ounces (370 g) peas (about 2½ cups), frozen or fresh

1 pound (454 g) pasta of choice

10 mint leaves

2 tablespoons olive oil

1 tablespoon lemon juice

2 garlic cloves

1 teaspoon salt, plus more for the pasta water

½ teaspoon red pepper flakes

½ cup (60 g) grated Parmesan, plus more for serving

1. Thinly slice the radishes with a mandoline or the slicer side of a box grater. Cut the slices into thin strips. Set aside.

2. Bring a small pot of water to a boil. Add the peas and cook until tender, 3 to 4 minutes. Drain.

3. Bring a pot of salted water to a boil. Cook the pasta according to recipe or package directions.

4. Meanwhile, place the peas, mint, olive oil, lemon juice, garlic, salt, and red pepper flakes in a food processor and puree until smooth.

5. Transfer the pea puree to a large saucepan and turn the heat to low to let simmer while the pasta cooks. When the pasta is almost done, stir ¼ cup (60 ml) of pasta water into the pea puree. Then add the Parmesan and mix until it's melted into the sauce.

6. When the pasta is done, drain, then add to the saucepan and stir to combine.

7. Serve with sliced radishes and additional Parmesan sprinkled on top if desired.

PAIRS WELL WITH: *Farfalle* (page 107), *Garganelli* (page 108), *Fusi Istriani* (page 111), *Cavatelli* (page 117), *Long Farfalle* (page 143), *Candy* (page 148), *Pinwheels* (page 151).

FOOD HISTORY

Parmigiano Reggiano is named for the two areas of Northern Italy where it's produced, Parma and Reggio Emilia, and is believed to date back to the Middle Ages. It's called the "King of Cheese" due to its complex, salty taste and its use as a flavor enhancer in dishes ranging from soups and pasta to potatoes and more.

Caprese Sauce with Roasted Tomatoes and Balsamic Glaze

PREP TIME 10 MIN | COOK TIME 35 MIN | 4 to 6 SERVINGS

I grew up in a family of beachgoers. Nearly every summer, we'd pile into the car and drive to the Jersey Shore, where we'd spend all day building sandcastles and playing in the waves. After long days of sun and sand, my dad would go to the kitchen to whip up a big platter of antipasti. There were always meats and cheeses, artichoke hearts, and a plate of Caprese salad—a simple combination of tomatoes, mozzarella, and basil, lightly seasoned and drizzled with olive oil. This combination just screams summer to me. I've tried to recreate those flavors here, with a simple sauce that really lets the ingredients shine.

1 cup (240 ml) balsamic vinegar

¼ cup (50 g) light brown sugar

1½ pounds (680 g) plum tomatoes

2 tablespoons olive oil, plus more for drizzling

1 teaspoon salt, divided, plus more for the pasta water

½ teaspoon black pepper

1 teaspoon thyme leaves

1 pound (454 g) pasta of choice

8 ounces (226 g) fresh mozzarella, diced into ½-inch (1 cm) cubes

¼ cup (15 g) basil leaves, thinly sliced

1. Preheat the oven to 425°F (220°C).

2. To make the balsamic glaze, bring the balsamic vinegar and brown sugar to a boil in a small saucepan. Lower the heat to medium-low and let simmer until the liquid has reduced by half, about 30 minutes. Transfer to a heat-safe cup or bowl and place it in the refrigerator to allow it to thicken.

3. Cut the tomatoes into quarters, then cut the quarters in half. Place them in a bowl and toss with olive oil, ½ teaspoon salt, pepper, and thyme leaves. Transfer to a baking sheet and cook until the tomatoes lose moisture and the skin shrivels, 25 to 30 minutes (see Tip).

4. Meanwhile, bring a pot of salted water to a boil. Cook the pasta according to recipe or package directions. Drain and set aside.

5. Combine the tomatoes, mozzarella, and basil in a large bowl. Drizzle on the olive oil and sprinkle with ½ teaspoon salt. Add the pasta and toss to combine.

6. Serve with balsamic glaze drizzled on top.

PAIRS WELL WITH: *Ravioli* (page 122), *Cestini* (page 129), *Caramelle* (page 134), *Four-Petal Flowers* (page 140), *Cookie Cutter Ravioli* (page 158), *Fruits and Vegetables* (page 170), *Witch Hats and Santa Hats* (page 177).

TIP

If you have the time, cook the tomatoes for 2 hours at 300°F (150°C) instead. The longer cooking time and lower temperature will bring out more of their natural sweetness.

FOOD HISTORY

Caprese salad hails from the island of Capri, where it's believed that a patriotic bricklayer came up with the dish after World War I to celebrate the colors of the Italian flag.

Pizza Pasta

PREP TIME 10 MIN | COOK TIME 45 MIN | 4 to 6 SERVINGS

When I lived in New York City for law school, there was a place near campus that had the largest slices of pizza I've ever seen. I'm talking three times larger than a normal slice. The place was always filled with students on Fridays at midnight, and I've never had a bite of pizza quite as satisfying as one of those after a long night out with friends. I don't make pizza nearly as much as I make pasta, so I like to incorporate classic pizza flavors in this dish here. Feel free to speed this recipe up by using 2 cups (450 g) of your favorite tomato sauce instead of making your own.

One 28-ounce (794 g) can whole San Marzano tomatoes

1 small palmful (about ¼ cup/15 g) basil leaves

¼ cup (60 ml) olive oil, divided

2 tablespoons tomato paste

1 garlic clove

1 teaspoon salt, plus more for the pasta water

½ pound (227 g) baby bella or white mushrooms, sliced

¼ teaspoon black pepper

1 cup (150 g) pepperoni slices, halved

½ cup (60 g) grated Parmesan

2 teaspoons oregano leaves, roughly chopped

1 pound (454 g) pasta of choice

1 cup (120 g) shredded fresh mozzarella

1. Puree the tomatoes, basil, 2 tablespoons olive oil, tomato paste, garlic, and salt in a blender until smooth.

2. Pour the tomato mixture into a wide saucepan and turn the heat to medium until the mixture comes to a boil, about 5 minutes. Reduce the heat to medium-low and let simmer until the tomatoes have reduced into a thick sauce, about 30 minutes, stirring occasionally.

3. Meanwhile, heat 2 tablespoons of olive oil in a separate skillet over medium heat. Stir in the mushrooms and sprinkle with salt and pepper. Cook until the mushrooms are browned, 4 to 5 minutes, stirring occasionally. Set aside.

4. When the tomato sauce is done cooking, taste and add more salt if necessary. Then add the mushrooms, pepperoni, Parmesan, and oregano and stir to combine.

5. Bring a pot of salted water to a boil, then cook the pasta according to recipe or package directions. Drain, then add the pasta to the sauce. Stir in the mozzarella.

6. Serve with additional Parmesan and oregano leaves sprinkled on top if desired.

PAIRS WELL WITH: *Farfalle* (page 107), *Garganelli* (page 108), *Funghetti* (page 114), *Cavatelli* (page 117), *Four-Petal Flowers* (page 140), *Witch Hats and Santa Hats* (page 177).

FOOD HISTORY

Modern pizza comes from Naples, where flatbreads with toppings were a common food for working-class people who needed easy nourishment in the 1700s and 1800s. They might be surprised at how far pizza has come, from the thin-crust New York slice to the deep-dish Chicago style to the thick square slices from Detroit.

CHAPTER EIGHT

Fillings

One of my hopes for this book is that you'll find the same joy and fun in pasta making that I do. Fresh pasta tastes amazing, and with the colors and patterns in this book, you'll be making some truly photo-worthy food. But ultimately, it's about more than just the final product, and the process to get there is equally important. This might be something you do with your friends or family, or a project you take on as your own. You might be content to stick to classic dough or try a color or two, or push yourself to make more complex patterns and shapes. No matter what, I hope you've had fun working through the doughs, patterns, and shapes in the previous chapters. We've now reached the final part that brings it all together: fillings.

It's not a big surprise that cuisines from all over the world include some form of filled pasta or dumpling, as there's something so satisfying about biting into a little pocket of meats, cheeses, or vegetables wrapped in pasta. With a good filling, you don't need much else, and I often eat ravioli with just a small amount of a butter, cream, or tomato sauce on top. Ravioli is also one of my daughter's favorites, and I use cookie cutters to make them into different, fun shapes (see Cookie Cutter Ravioli, page 158).

Each of the eight recipes in this chapter produces enough filling for one batch of pasta and is fairly simple to make, but the flavors come through strongly. With a beautiful striped tortellini or a vibrant sunflower ravioli, sometimes a simple filling is exactly what you need!

Ricotta and Pecorino Filling

PREP TIME 10 MIN | COOK TIME 40 MIN | MAKES 2½ CUPS (450 G) | 4 to 6 SERVINGS

This is the filling I use most often when making ravioli. It's rich, tasty, and (if you use store-bought ricotta) very fast to make. But if you've never made ricotta from scratch before, I encourage you to give it a try. People are often surprised at how easy it is to make, and the result is creamier and fresher than the kind that comes in a plastic tub. It's also incredibly tasty on its own—drizzle it with honey and spread it on toast or throw some into a salad. You'll need some cheesecloth (an extra-fine strainer is a decent substitute) and a little bit of time, but it's just a few simple ingredients.

8 cups (1.9 L) whole milk

1½ teaspoons salt, divided

3 tablespoons white wine vinegar

¼ cup (30 g) grated Pecorino Romano

2 teaspoons lemon juice

½ teaspoon black pepper

1. To make the ricotta, pour the milk into a large saucepan. Add 1 teaspoon salt and cook over medium heat, stirring occasionally, until the temperature reaches 185°F (85°C) and the milk is just beginning to bubble, 10 to 15 minutes.

2. Turn off the heat. Leave the pan on the burner and stir in the vinegar. Let sit for 20 minutes without touching it. You'll notice that the milk quickly curdles (the solid curds separate from the liquid whey).

3. Meanwhile, line a colander with three layers of a cheesecloth, making sure that the cloth is large enough to hang off the edges. Place the colander in a large bowl.

4. Use a large slotted spoon to scoop the solid curds out of the pan and transfer them to the cheesecloth. Keep scooping until only the liquid whey remains in the pan (see Tip 1).

5. The ricotta is ready to eat right away, but it will be rather moist. Before you fill your pasta, let the ricotta drain for 20 to 30 minutes until it's no longer visibly wet (see Tip 2).

6. To make the filling, transfer the ricotta to a large bowl and add the Pecorino, lemon juice, pepper, and the remaining ½ teaspoon of salt (see Tip 3). Give everything a good mix.

7. The filling should be cohesive but not runny, and you should be able to pick up a spoonful without it falling apart. If it's very dry, stir in a spoonful of milk.

FOOD HISTORY

The word *ricotta* means "recooked" in Italian, and it's traditionally made by recooking liquid whey, a byproduct of making cheese. Today, it's more commonly made at home using whole milk or cream as a starter instead.

TIPS

1. Be careful not to dump the entire pan of curds and whey into the cheesecloth; the excess liquid will clog it up.
2. You can speed up this process by giving the cheesecloth a good squeeze.
3. If using store-bought ricotta, use 1½ to 2 cups (360 to 420 g) in place of your homemade ricotta.

Butternut Squash, Sage, and Nutmeg Filling

PREP TIME 10 MIN | COOK TIME 45 MIN | MAKES 3 CUPS (750 G) | 4 to 6 SERVINGS

Butternut squash already tastes like fall, but why not really play into the autumn vibes and add some sage and nutmeg as well? Or, at this point, should we just go all the way and make a pumpkin spice latte filling (don't tempt me)? You can pair this with my Creamy Butternut Squash Sauce with Roasted Shallots and Garlic (page 199) if you're a big squash fan, but I think all this filling really needs is a little brown butter spooned over the top. That and a nice mug of hot apple cider.

1 medium butternut squash (about 2½ pounds/1.2 kg), halved vertically (see Tip), seeds removed

1 tablespoon olive oil

1 teaspoon salt

½ teaspoon black pepper

2 tablespoons unsalted butter, softened

½ cup (130 g) ricotta

5 to 7 fresh sage leaves

⅛ teaspoon ground nutmeg

1. Preheat oven to 400°F (200°C). Line a baking sheet with parchment paper.

2. Place the squash halves, cut side up, on the baking sheet.

3. Drizzle with olive oil, then rub the oil into the squash so the entire cut side is covered. Sprinkle with salt and pepper.

4. Roast for 35 to 40 minutes, until the squash is tender enough to pierce with a fork. Remove from the oven and let cool.

5. When it's cool enough to touch, scoop the insides of the squash into a food processor (discard the peel). Add the remaining ingredients, along with a pinch of salt and pepper, and blend until smooth.

TIP

If the squash is difficult to cut, pierce it with a knife several times and microwave for 3 to 4 minutes. This should soften the skin enough to make it easier to cut.

PASTA HISTORY

Depending on where you are in Italy, the terms *tortelli* and *ravioli* might be used to describe filled pasta. In the 1960s, Italian cookbooks sometimes differentiated by using *tortelli* to refer to squash-filled pasta and *ravioli* to refer to ricotta-filled pastas.

Spinach-Ricotta Filling

PREP TIME 10 MIN | COOK TIME 5 MIN | MAKES 2½ CUPS (625 G) | 4 to 6 SERVINGS

There's a reason spinach and ricotta are a classic combination for Ravioli (page 122), Tortellini (page 125), and other filled pastas. This filling is straightforward to make yet full of flavor—creamy, cheesy, and hearty all in one. Italians often use it as the base for *ravioli di magro*, a meatless meal served on Fridays during Lent, but I certainly think it's worthy of eating all year long. You can use homemade ricotta (see Ricotta and Pecorino Filling, page 220) or the store-bought kind.

2 tablespoons unsalted butter

2 garlic cloves, crushed or minced

9 ounces (250 g) spinach

1½ cups (400 g) ricotta

¼ cup (30 g) grated Pecorino Romano

1 tablespoon lemon juice

½ teaspoon salt, plus more to taste

½ teaspoon black pepper, plus more to taste

1. Melt the butter in a large skillet over medium heat, then stir in the garlic and cook until lightly browned, about 1 minute. Stir in the spinach and cook until most of the leaves are wilted, about 2 minutes.

2. Transfer the spinach to a colander. When it's cool enough to touch, squeeze out any excess liquid with your hands and finely chop the spinach.

3. Transfer to a large bowl, then add the ricotta, Pecorino, lemon juice, salt, and pepper. Taste and add more salt or pepper as desired. Alternatively, you can blend the ingredients together in a food processor until smooth.

FOOD FACT

Ricotta has been made in Italy since at least 1000 BCE, when cheese makers began using rennet to produce hard cheeses that could be preserved for long periods of time. This increase in cheese production led to a lot of leftover whey, which in turn was used to make ricotta.

Mushroom Filling with Shallots and Mascarpone

PREP TIME 5 MIN | COOK TIME 10 MIN | MAKES 2½ CUPS (550 G) | 4 to 6 SERVINGS

As a kid, I wasn't a fan of mushrooms, eating around them on the plate and picking them off pizza. But now I've come to appreciate their earthy umami flavor. This filling allows the sauteed mushroom flavor to shine through but combines it with some fresh parsley, sweet mascarpone cheese, and shallots. The filling adds a richness to any pasta dish; it pairs well with Brown Butter with Toasted Hazelnuts and Sage (page 184) or Garlic Cream Sauce with Pancetta and Crispy Shallots (page 188).

2 tablespoons olive oil

2 shallots, chopped

1 pound (454 g) white mushrooms, sliced

2 to 3 garlic cloves, sliced

1 teaspoon salt

½ teaspoon black pepper

¼ cup (30 g) grated Parmesan

¼ cup (60 g) mascarpone

2 tablespoons chopped parsley

1. Heat the olive oil in a skillet or frying pan over medium heat and then add the shallots. Cook until wilted and starting to brown, about 4 minutes.

2. Add the mushrooms and garlic along with the salt and pepper. Sauté until the mushrooms are tender and brown, about 5 minutes (see Tip).

3. Transfer the mixture to a food processor. Add the Parmesan, mascarpone, and parsley and puree until smooth.

TIP

If your mushrooms look too dry, you may need to add more olive oil to the pan so they don't burn.

FOOD FACT

Mascarpone hails from Northern Italy and is often used in desserts like tiramisu, cannoli, and cheesecake due to its sweet, creamy flavor.

Pepperoni Pizza Filling

PREP TIME 5 MIN | MAKES 3 CUPS (500 G) | 4 to 6 SERVINGS

Nothing will ever top pasta as my favorite food, of course, but pizza is a regular staple of my diet. This filling embodies the essence of a good slice of pepperoni pizza, wrapped up in a little bundle of pasta dough. It's best to roll the dough as thinly as possible for this filling so your ravioli doesn't have to cook for too long; we're looking for perfectly cooked mozzarella that stretches and pulls as you bite into it. This filling won't be as compact as some of the ricotta-based ones, so use a spoon instead of a piping bag to add it to your dough.

1 cup (150 g) sliced pepperoni

1 cup (120 g) shredded fresh mozzarella

½ cup (60 g) grated Parmesan

½ teaspoon dried oregano

¾ cup (185 g) Weeknight Tomato Sauce (page 192) or store-bought tomato sauce

1. Cut the pepperoni slices into ¼-inch (6 mm) pieces.

2. Mix the mozzarella, Parmesan, pepperoni, and oregano in a large bowl until well combined.

3. Stir in the tomato sauce.

4. Cover the bowl and place in the refrigerator for about 1 hour before using. This will help solidify the filling and make it easier to scoop.

FOOD HISTORY

Although pizza has existed in the United States since at least the early 1900s, it was mostly eaten by Italian immigrants until after World War II, when returning soldiers brought back a love for the food. Pepperoni was added by Italian immigrants in New York City, because it cures much faster than other meats, like capicola, and therefore was cheaper and more accessible to a working-class budget.

Sauteed Eggplant and Tomato Filling

PREP TIME 15 MIN | COOK TIME 15 MIN | MAKES 2½ CUPS (650 G) | 4 to 6 SERVINGS

Many traditional ravioli recipes are heavy on the cheese and meat (not that I'm complaining!), but this filling is completely vegan. It's my take on a traditional Sicilian dish called *pasta alla Norma*, a popular recipe that's basically a tomato sauce tossed with sauteed eggplant. It's typically garnished with ricotta salata, a firmer version of fresh ricotta made from sheep's milk, but I leave that out here. I use fresh basil, but other herbs like oregano or parsley would also work well.

2 tablespoons olive oil

1 medium eggplant (about 1¼ pound/550 g), diced into ½-inch (6 mm) cubes

2 garlic cloves, crushed or minced

1 teaspoon salt

½ teaspoon red pepper flakes, optional

1 cup (250 g) Weeknight Tomato Sauce (page 192) or store-bought tomato sauce

1 small palmful (about ¼ cup/15 g) basil leaves, julienned

1. Heat the oil over medium heat in a large skillet. Add the eggplant, garlic, salt, and red pepper flakes, if using. Stir frequently until the eggplant is tender, about 10 minutes (see Tip). Remove the eggplant and pat dry with a paper towel to remove any excess oil.

2. When the eggplant has cooled to the touch, mash with a fork or puree in a food processor for about 15 seconds.

3. Combine the eggplant, tomato sauce, and basil in a large bowl. Taste and add more salt or red pepper flakes if necessary.

TIP

There's a great debate about whether it's necessary to salt eggplant before sautéing to reduce the bitterness and remove excess water, leading to a crispier texture. Since we don't need a crispy texture for this filling, I usually skip this step, but you are free to try and see if you notice a difference. Cut the eggplant into cubes or slices and toss them in a large bowl with a generous amount of salt. Place a heavy bowl or plate on top of the eggplant; before long, you'll notice water dripping off the pieces. Let sit for about an hour, then rinse the eggplant thoroughly with cold water. Dry with a kitchen towel before using.

PASTA HISTORY

Pasta alla Norma was named in honor of Italian composer Vincenzo Bellini and his famous opera, *Norma*. The story goes that poet and writer Nino Martoglio tried the dish and declared "This is a real Norma," meaning it was a masterpiece, and the name stuck.

Italian Sausage Filling

PREP TIME 5 MIN | COOK TIME 20 MIN | MAKES 2½ CUPS (500 G) | 4 to 6 SERVINGS

Meat fillings are an important part of the Italian pasta-making tradition, and classics like Ravioli (page 122) and Tortellini (page 125) are often filled with some combination of ground beef, pork loin, prosciutto, and more. This recipe keeps it simple, using sweet Italian sausage that comes already seasoned with fennel, garlic, onions, and other spices. The "sweet" in sweet Italian sausage doesn't actually mean these are sugary; it simply means they're a milder version of spicy Italian sausage and contain some sweet basil. Feel free to use the spicier version if you prefer.

2 tablespoons olive oil

1 medium yellow onion, chopped

1 pound (454 g) ground sweet Italian sausage

2 garlic cloves, sliced

1 teaspoon salt

½ teaspoon black pepper

¼ cup (30 g) grated Parmesan

¼ cup (65 g) ricotta

2 tablespoons chopped parsley

½ teaspoon fennel seeds

1. Heat the olive oil in a skillet over medium heat. Add the onion and cook until translucent, about 8 minutes, stirring occasionally.

2. Add the sausage and garlic. Sprinkle with salt and pepper.

3. Break the meat up with a spatula and cook until it is no longer pink, 10 minutes, stirring occasionally.

4. Transfer to a food processor and add the Parmesan, ricotta, parsley, and fennel seeds. Puree until smooth.

FOOD HISTORY

Pork is a common ingredient in Italian cooking, with such a wide variety of dried and cured pork products like salami, prosciutto, mortadella, and capocollo (which you may know by the Italian-American pronunciation gabagool), to name a few.

Beet and Goat Cheese Filling

PREP TIME 10 MIN | COOK TIME 45 MIN | MAKES 2½ CUPS (600 G) | 4 to 6 SERVINGS

This book is all about using bright colors in pasta making, so of course that extends to the filling, too! Beets have a magnificent natural color, a vibrant purplish magenta that brightens up any plate. Even with the addition of goat cheese, this filling retains the beautiful beet color, so I love to use it with Classic Pasta Dough (page 38). If you roll the dough thinly enough, the reddish color will shine through, and you'll have stunning pasta without too much effort.

3 large red beets (about 1⅔ pounds/750 g), stems removed (see Tip 1)

8 ounces (227 g) goat cheese

1 garlic clove

1 teaspoon salt

2 teaspoons lemon juice

Leaves from 3 thyme sprigs

1. Preheat the oven to 400°F (200°C).

2. Place the beets on a baking sheet and cook for about 45 minutes, or until fork-tender.

3. Remove from the oven and let cool. Once the beets are cool enough to touch, peel and transfer to a food processor.

4. Add the cheese, garlic, salt, lemon juice, and thyme leaves. Puree until smooth (see Tip 2).

TIPS

1. If you're short on time, feel free to use precooked beets or canned beets, which are usually readily available at the grocery store.

2. If the puree is too watery, place it in the fridge for 30 minutes or until it solidifies.

Index

Acknowledgments

This book would not exist without the incredible group of pasta lovers who follow @DannyLovesPasta, who have supported, nurtured, and inspired me along my journey from lawyer to chef to cookbook author. It's because of this community that I first started experimenting with color, trying new ingredients, and inventing new shapes, and you've pushed me out of my comfort zone to be more creative, more expressive, and more heartfelt. I am truly grateful for each one of you, and all you've done to change my life in ways I never expected.

This book would also not be possible without the endless love and support from my husband Steve, my partner and best friend for the last 15 years. Steve, I can't even describe how much you mean to me; thank you for the love, guidance, and enthusiasm you have shown me countless times. On our wedding day we said, "I promise to respect and honor you, care for you with tenderness, and support you with patience and love. I will always love you." Those words are still incredibly true.

I could never express how blessed I am by my family, who have been a constant source of love and support since the day I was born. To my parents, thank you for always loving and believing in me; you gave me the perfect, solid ground on which to build my life and made me the person I am today. You've always loved me for exactly who I am and always made me feel special, and for that I'm eternally grateful. I love you so much.

I talk a lot in this book about the great impact my grandmother had on my life, but my grandfather is equally as impactful. Thank you, Grampa, for your years of wisdom and love, and for always being

there for me. I often think about the lessons you've taught me and the example you set by living your life with integrity and compassion. You are one of my greatest inspirations, and I'm so lucky for the lifetime of memories you and Nanny gave me.

To Nick and Jason, I feel so lucky to have two brothers who are also such great friends of mine, and I'm so grateful to both of you. Thank you for always being there for me and showing me nothing but kindness and love. To Tricia, Laura, Dan, Julia, Natalie, Tyler, Sienna, Jack, and Sam, I love you all and am so happy to have you in my life.

To my mother- and father-in-law, thank you for welcoming me into the family from day one and always believing in me. Your support means so much to me.

To my aunts, uncles, and cousins, this book is a celebration of our traditions, holidays, and family. Thank you for all the memories you've given me and all the love you've shown me.

I could not have written this book without the help of everyone who took care of my daughter and watched her while I worked. I'm so lucky to have you all in my life and so grateful. Thank you to my parents, my in-laws, Lorraine, Lorena, Nick, Kirti, Deepa, Rajive, and Jenni. And thank you, Jenni, for our years of friendship; it means so much to me.

I'm grateful to everyone at Manhattan Legal Services, who are doing incredibly important work under difficult conditions with not nearly enough recognition. Thank you for the years of mentorship and support and for allowing me to take time to spend with my daughter, which ultimately led to the creation of this book. Thank you to Peggy, Roz, Shantonu, Dao, Ami, and so many others.

Writing and publishing this book was truly a team effort, and it would not have happened without the amazing people working with me. Thank you so much to my agent, Stephanie Winter, for finding me and helping me realize I could write a cookbook. I'm so grateful for your kindness, expertise, and support, and this book could not have happened without you. You were instrumental in shaping the direction of this book, and I'm so thankful for you.

I'm so fortunate to work with my amazing editor, Olivia Peluso. I've learned so much about writing and recipe development from you, and this book is infinitely better thanks to your hard work. Thank you for your incredibly helpful guidance and edits, and for keeping me on track. And thank you to Chris Stolle for getting this project off the ground and helping it take shape.

I could not imagine a better art director to work with than Jessica Lee. Jessica, I'm blown away by your talent and vision, and I'll be forever grateful for your work on this book. Every page you designed and photograph you set up made this a better book, and I owe you so much.

Thank you so much to my photographer, Rikki Snyder. Seeing your photos of my pasta for the first time was something I'll never forget, and you made them look better than I ever could. From the very first photo, I knew I was in good hands, and that you were the perfect person to work with.

Thank you to my food stylist, Leslie Orlandini; I could not have made it through the photoshoot

without your expertise, help, and support. You made every photo better, and I'm so lucky to have had you work on this book.

Thank you to Rebecca Miller Ffrench and The Upstate Table for letting me use your beautiful space for my photoshoot; it was the perfect setting for the shoot, and your kindness and hospitality are so appreciated.

Thank you to Trish Sebben Malone for testing each of these recipes and providing invaluable feedback.

Thank you so much to Bill Thomas, Mike Sanders, and everyone at DK and Penguin Random House for taking a chance on me and helping me bring this book to fruition.

And finally, to Ezzie: I love you more than I can say, and you've brought me more joy than you can know. You kept me going when I was ready to give up and energized me when I thought I had no energy left. You're my everything.

About the Author

Danny Freeman is a chef and content creator known for his colorful and creative takes on fresh pasta and Italian cooking. He fell in love with pasta making after attempting one of his grandmother's recipes but quickly veered from the traditional and began making pasta in bright colors and original shapes. After posting videos of his pasta creations online, he gained a devoted following and developed his signature style of colorful, joyful, and delicious food. His work has been featured by *Good Morning America, The Rachael Ray Show, Teen Vogue*, Buzzfeed, and more, and his videos have been viewed hundreds of millions of times. A graduate of Tufts University and Columbia Law School, he was a legal services lawyer before becoming a pasta chef. Danny lives in New York's Hudson Valley with his husband and their daughter. He can be found on TikTok, Instagram, and YouTube under the name @DannyLovesPasta.